Pip Barker started working life as a teacher in a comprehensive school and later moved on to work for social services as a care home manager and later as an inspector of care homes under the Quality Care Commission. He has now retired.

Pip has always taken a keen interest in local history and has linked this with collecting postcards and other ephemera. His first visit to Princetown came as a result of discovering that his great-grandfather was a warder at the prison.

Following his move to Dartmoor in 2014, he quickly became involved with the Dartmoor Prison Museum and undertook responsibility for archiving. Such is his interest that he now delivers talks to local groups on all things related to Dartmoor Prison.

To all those who have contributed to our local history and
continue to do so.

Pip Barker

PRINCETOWN AND THE CONSCIENTIOUS OBJECTORS OF WW1

AUSTIN MACAULEY PUBLISHERS™

LONDON • CAMBRIDGE • NEW YORK • SHARJAH

A CIP catalogue record for this title is available from the British Library.

ISBN 9781398419780 (Paperback)
ISBN 9781398419810 (ePub e-book)

www.austinmacauley.com

First Published (2021)
Austin Macauley Publishers Ltd
25 Canada Square
Canary Wharf
London
E14 5LQ

My thanks to the governor of Dartmoor Prison and the staff of Dartmoor Prison Museum, particularly Brian Dingle and Graham Edmondson, for supporting me with this project and for making available some of the material used in this book. This material included the accounts of Roland and Sidney Reigne, William Ralph Done, Alfred Downs and James Butcher, all Conscientious Objectors at Dartmoor, sections of which I have quoted. My thanks extend to their families who supplied their written accounts to the museum.

I would also like to thank my good friend, David Garner, who undertook to read my work and who offered constructive comments.

Finally, I would like to thank my wife, Gill, for without her support, help and encouragement in this project, this story would have remained untold.

Dartmoor Work Centre
1917–1919

Introduction

Neither the length of the War nor the tremendous number of casualties was foreseen when the first World War broke out on July 28, 1914.

In the words of many at the time, the prediction was that it would be 'over by Christmas' and volunteers rushed to do their bit in case they were too late to take part. No one realised at the time the military capabilities and weaponry of the German Army which was to cause such devastating numbers of dead and injured. Such were the losses that the British Government could no longer rely on volunteers to fill the dwindling ranks of our own military. By 1916, action needed to be taken, so the Military Service Act was introduced in January of that year. This required that all single men or widowers between the ages of 18 and 41 must enlist. Those that did not fall into this category were free to carry on with their normal everyday life until 25 May when the requirement to enlist was extended to include married men. From this time, the only men in the 18–41 age group not to be conscripted were those in reserved occupations.

There were, however, some men who refused to enlist or fight and became known as Conscientious Objectors. By their refusal they were contravening the terms of the Military Service Act.

Provision needed to be made for these men for the duration of the War, and the initial solution was to send them to prisons as common criminals. Later, some were offered the opportunity to live in work camps and carry out work that the government described as of 'National Importance'.

One such work camp proposed was in Princetown, Devon on the site of the former Dartmoor Convict Prison. Originally opened in 1809 to house French prisoners of war from the Napoleonic Wars and later in 1813 American prisoners from the War of 1812, it was a forbidding granite construction 1500 feet above sea level in a very hostile environment. Later in 1850 it became a Convict Prison, housing some of the most dangerous men in the country. All the inhabitants of Princetown relied on Dartmoor Prison for their livelihood. This Act of 1916 was to change the lives of those very people.

Men seeking exemption from military service had to put their case before a tribunal, Tavistock being the nearest one to Princetown. The tribunal consisted of older men, many veterans of the Boer War, and so the COs entreaties were viewed on the whole unsympathetically. A large number were shipped to regiments where they refused to participate in any activity associated with the War. Some refused to put on the uniform and there are many stories of men being marched naked around parade grounds.

Two Conscientious Objectors who eventually ended up at Dartmoor Work Centre, as Dartmoor Prison later became known, were Bernard Bonner, a watchmaker by trade, and Harry Stanton, a bank official and quaker. Both had refused to don uniform and engage in any activities to help the War effort.

Despite being threatened and bullied, they were sent to the Eastern Non-Combatant Corps at Landguard Camp in Felixstowe. Bonner was sentenced to death on 10 June, 1916, but the sentence was commuted immediately to ten years' Penal Servitude.

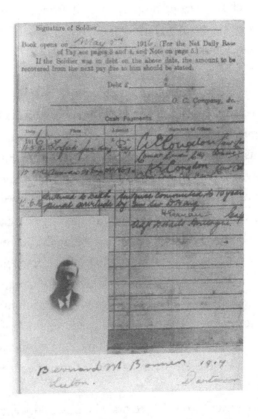

Postcard of Bernard Bonner's Army Service Record

Later that year, the Home Office Committee for the Employment of Conscientious Objectors (HOCECO) was set up to undertake 'Work of National Importance' not associated with the War. The work consisted of land reclamation and road building. It was regarded as work that helped local communities rather than the War effort. The first camp setup was in Scotland at Dyce near Aberdeen. This camp only lasted three months due to the appalling conditions where over 250 men lived in tents that had been used in the Boer War some 20 years earlier. The damp and rain made conditions for work in the nearby quarry intolerable, and after a few deaths the camp was closed down.

It was announced in Parliament on Wednesday, 21 February, 1917, by Sir George Cave, Secretary of State for the Home Department, that:

"Dartmoor Prison shall cease to be used as a prison, and shall be handed over for the duration of the War to the HOCECO. The men who will be sent there by the committee will be employed on the large farm attached to the prison, and on the reclamation for agricultural purposes of neighbouring portions of Dartmoor. The men will live and work under conditions similar to those in force at the committee's establishments at Wakefield and Warwick. It is hoped that the buildings may be ready for the reception of the Conscientious Objectors in about a fortnight's time. It is intended that the building should revert to the purpose of a prison after the War." (COs' Hansard No 20, March 1, 1917).

So, on March 8, 1917, Dartmoor Prison opened its doors for the arrival of the first group of Conscientious Objectors.

From Prison to Work Centre

Dartmoor was closed as a prison in February 1917. At this time, convicts who were not considered to be dangerous were offered the opportunity to fight for their country, provided they were between 18 and 41 years. 80% took this option. The remainder were sent to other prisons in the UK. The preparations needed to transition Dartmoor Prison into Dartmoor Work Centre; Princetown began immediately and as announced by Sir George Cave, preparations were expected to take 'about a fortnight'.

On completion of this work, COs began to arrive from other prisons. Initial impressions from the men's point of view were a fairly welcoming one. Arriving by train, Roland Reigne, *observing the surrounding view, wrote:*

"We were about 1,400ft. above sea level, and the great expanse of moorland seemed strange after the much-restricted views in prison."

At the station they found that:

"There were lots of people waiting for us, and they offered to carry our bundles to the prison, half-a-mile away." (James Butcher)

On walking from the station to the prison they passed some large granite buildings about which Roland Reigne remarked that they: "Seemed cold and uninviting, somewhat akin to a prison block, so what of the prison itself?"

He answered his own question on entering the prison gates for the first time by remarking that the prison halls were:

"Grey and cold looking, the whole place could only be described as grim."

The outside appearance of the prison was somewhat tempered by the welcome that he found inside amongst existing members of the settlement's CO community. *He further remarked:*

"After the official reception, we were approached by 2 COs who addressed us as Comrade and invited us to accompany them to the kitchen. There, on a large, white scrubbed table the Cook brought us a meal, during which we were plied with no end of questions as how we had fared; at the same time, they made us feel very welcome."

Within a fortnight of its opening, there were already 407 occupants. This number increased to 582 by the end of the month, and by the 19th April there were 856 inhabitants. Eventually, the number rose to 1200.

The Kitchen

Prison Laundry

Two of the original occupants were George and Fred Nunn who came from Stanford-le-Hope in Essex. Writing to his mother on 14 March, 1917, George tells her that their luggage has not yet arrived and that Fred is the foreman in the laundry.

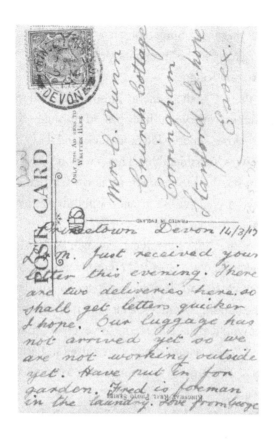

George Nunn's postcard to his mother

First and foremost, as the concept of a prison had needed to be changed to more open accommodation for reception of these COs, all locks on cell doors were disabled—a matter of some surprise to the incoming men. Eric Dott, CO, wrote:

"At first I was a little surprised to find it was a proper prison where we were to stay—but I was soon put alright about that... I went to my cell, which we prefer to call a "room" and I found that all the doors have their locks screwed up and that there is nothing to keep us in our rooms."

The contrast to his previous prison life was remarked upon by Roland Reigne:

"For the COs, the general atmosphere and conditions were different; everyone had passed through the prison system of close supervision and lock and key. Here, the difference was considerable. There was no restriction on going from one hall to another, so if we felt that we would like to have a chat with a friend or fellow settler, we just strolled round hoping to find him in."

Some of the more sensitive areas such as the chain room where handcuffs, body belts and other forms of restraint were stored, were closed off. It was envisioned that under the new usage of the buildings, with COs instead of prisoners, no types of restraint would ever be needed. However, at some point the COs gained access as questions were raised in Parliament on 7 June, 1917 about pre-war punishments to convicts and, as Mr Jowett asked:

"As to whether he (referring to Mr W Brace, Under Secretary at the Home Office) was aware that COs, now detained at Dartmoor, have inspected these instruments?" (COs' Hansard No 31, question raised by Mr Jowett, MP)

Other evidence of the COs' access is seen in a photograph taken at the time of a man posing in a canvas straight jacket.

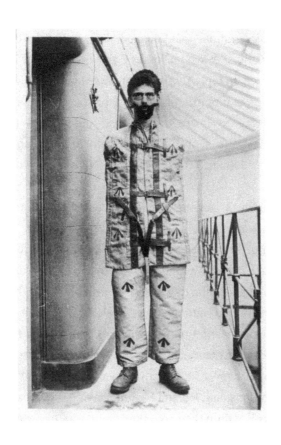

CO posing in a strait jacket

There was accommodation for 1200 men, so the question of staffing also had to be addressed. Prison Warders were not exempt from the terms of the Military Service Act of 1916 and its subsequent update in May of that year, so men who were between the ages of 18 and 41 years would no longer serve at the work centre. This eventually left only 57 staff members to run the work centre under the authority of Major E R Reade, previously the governor who now became the manager. These 57 staff members encompassed office and staff administration, maintenance staff, medical officers as well as warders, of whom James Carr was the Chief Warder.

W Brace, in reply to a question raised in Parliament, said:

"The great majority of these are prison officers, and their functions are to instruct, supervise and control the men employed at the centre. Salaries paid to them amount to £8,167 per annum." (COs' Hansard No 47, 22 November, 1917)

These lower staffing levels were remarked upon by Eric Dott who wrote:

"I learned that there are only two or three warders in the whole place, that it is practically run by the COs themselves."

All evidence illustrates that Dartmoor Prison had now truly transformed into Dartmoor Work Centre; it was no longer a penal institution for criminals, but a much freer and more relaxed environment for the retention of Conscientious Objectors. However, it was still a place subject to disciplines and regulations, and Roland Reigne, having previously noted that the COs within their free time could mix freely and even walk out on the Moor, observed:

"However, the restrictions, buildings, warders, food and penal nature of the work kept one quite conscious of being a prisoner."

Life Inside Dartmoor Work Centre

Daily Routine

Although the Conscientious Objectors were not considered to be prisoners and had the freedom of not being locked in their rooms, they were still subject to an organised daily routine.

Their day started early to allow for ten hours work from Monday to Friday, and 6 ½ hours on Saturday. Sunday was a day of rest. During what free time they had, there were opportunities for socialisation—either visiting each other in their rooms or forming clubs and societies within the centre. There were opportunities to go outside the centre to visit the local village or ramble across the moor, but gates were locked at 9.30pm so all had to be back inside by that time.

Rations

Rations issued to the men were constantly under review. Questions were frequently raised in the House of Commons which were considered and answered by Sir George Cave, Secretary of State for the Home Department, the equivalent today of the Home Secretary, who announced on Monday, 12 March, 1917:

"The daily amounts of meat and bread to be issued to the Conscientious Objectors at Dartmoor are as follows: Meat 6oz; bread 9oz. Vegetarians will be allowed 5oz of bread per day extra. The amount of sugar issued will not exceed 12oz per man per week." (COs' Hansard No 23)

Less than a fortnight later, in response to a further question in the House of Commons, Sir George Cave announced the revised ration allowance as:

"Bread 9oz per day; meat 6oz per day; potatoes 8oz per week; jam 2oz per day; margarine ¾ oz per day; tea 1 pint per day."

This led to uproar and even more questions being raised by MPs who observed that COs were now receiving the same rations as soldiers employed on active service at the front.

Following further review, Mr W Brace, Under Secretary in the Home Department, issued a statement on 9 May revealing the current COs' allowances:

"The daily rations issued at the present time to the men employed at Princetown are as follows: Bread 9oz, meat 6ozs, uncooked including bone, tea, coffee or cocoa 2 pints, vegetables 8oz, pudding 8oz, margarine ¾ oz, jam 2oz, porridge 1 pint, soup 1 pint, cheese 2oz." (COs' Hansard No 30, May 24, 1917)

It is interesting to note the implication of diverse perceptions of the status of the Conscientious Objectors at Princetown. Whilst the MP's question about the rations issued being the same as soldiers at the front, Brace refers not to COs but 'men employed at Princetown'.

Occasionally, substitutions were made when items in the standard ration provision was not available; for example, dried fish could take the place of meat. Sometimes fruit was available in dried form, apricots in particular.

It is understandable that questions were raised with regard to the food rations. These men were viewed unsympathetically, and in some cases with open hostility, by ordinary members of the public who were losing loved ones daily through fighting at the front. Was it right or fair that those who refused to fight for their country should be fed as well as those who were living in such squalid and life-threatening conditions? A question that politicians needed to ask in order to address the feelings of many civilians who were also on reduced rations.

The mood of the people was summed up in an article published by the Western Times on October 16, 1917, which quoted the Chairman of the Tavistock Rural Tribunal, Mr F Nicholls, as saying, with regards to the men at Princetown:

"There are 1100 there absolutely wasting the food of this country."

This echoed the comments made by the Bishop of Exeter, Lord William Cecil, who during his preaching cited the refusal of the COs to gather the harvest which was now rotting in the fields:

"They can refuse because their rations are safe." (Liverpool Echo October 9, 1917)

In addition to their supplied food rations, COs had their own money which enabled them to buy extra food and even the privilege of going out for a meal.

The medical officer at the centre, Eric Battiscombe, noted in his journal dated September 9, 1918:

"Scores of the people living in the village have expressed sourness at the COs living here supplied with cheese, jam, dried fruits etc. when they were either unable to procure them as well or only at a prohibitive cost."

On the same date, Dr Battiscombe comments further as to rations being:

"Sufficient in quantity. At any rate, every man who has come from prison has gained weight during the first month: the average being about ½ stone."

This should be taken, however, in some context, especially with reference to those who came from prison. Rations there were meagre and meals less frequent, and some of these men had engaged in hunger strikes as a protest to being incarcerated. No reference is made to their weight on entering prison, and it would be reasonable to assume that their weight may well have dropped during their time there.

With reference to the Table of Weights, recorded in the medical journal, every man, including those who did not come from prison, gained weight, and none were recorded as losing weight. The conclusion of the medical officer therefore, that food rations were sufficient would be borne out by this evidence.

Although the War ended in November 1918, the COs remained in the Dartmoor Work Centre until April of the following year. As food became more plentiful, their rations were further increased, as shown in the journal entry dated March 26, 1919, by having 6ozs extra of flour per week and 5ozs extra vegetables daily, with a choice of potatoes, turnips, carrots or parsnips when available. The cost of this was an additional 4 ½d per head daily, but as meat had been reduced in price, the additional cost worked out as 2 ½d per day. This was the last entry to be recorded in the medical officer's journal with regards to rations.

Clothing

As these Conscientious Objectors were not classed as prisoners, there was no uniform for them to wear. When not working, they could wear their own clothes if they chose to; in fact, many were very smartly dressed, as evidenced in photographs taken at the time.

Some COs came from poor backgrounds, but no man was left in rags or inadequate clothing as all received government issue. Eric Dott, a CO, wrote:

"Last Friday I was fitted out with the 'Home Office' clothes—a tweed jacket and waistcoat, corduroy trousers, a good overcoat, warm flannelled drawers and vests and shirts, warm socks, strong boots, cloth cap and muffler and leather leggings, all good well-made clothes."

Not all the men were impressed with the clothes they were given before travelling to Dartmoor. William Done and his fellow COs at Wormwood Scrubs were issued cord trousers and Derby tweed jackets similar to those used in poor law workhouses.

Clothing appropriate to their daily tasks was also issued. Those working outside were given greatcoats or oilskins, and in winter, men working on the moor, for example, agricultural or quarry workers, would receive an extra cardigan, jersey or long-sleeved vest. This only applied to those doing physical work outside.

Eric Battiscombe, the medical officer, in his journal entry for October 19, 1917, remarked:

"The majority of the men do not require extra clothing, and included in these are all the delicate and weakly men who work indoors in the warm."

Some indoor working areas would generate heat such as the kitchen, laundry or the blacksmith's shop. However, there would be other areas, where although there were fires lit, these were not efficient in keeping at bay the cold and damp generated in a granite building. The dairy also would be a cold working place, albeit classed as an indoor occupation. Those working outside would most certainly need extra clothing, as although not always 'cold', the damp atmosphere combined with bitter winds on the exposed moorland would introduce a severe chill factor to the working day.

Still, these clothing provisions were questioned in the House of Commons as being over-generous. On April 23, 1917, Sir Kinloch-Cooke, MP for Devonport, in a speech to Parliament said:

"They are provided with every possible article of clothing necessary for their work, and are given every facility that can be possibly provided to do farm work. They work in overcoats so as not to get cold; they wear woollen gloves to prevent their hands getting red and they are given food which is as good, if not better, than our soldiers at the front." (COs' Hansard No 27, May 3, 1917).

Inside a Room

A typical room—no longer referred to as a cell—provided a temporary home for a Conscientious Objector. Basic furniture and bedding were supplied, but they were allowed to bring in their own comforts and articles for decoration. Personal possessions that men could bring into their rooms also included books. They weren't, however, allowed to bring in any pamphlets or materials dealing with Conscientious

Objector's beliefs or anything that could be considered to be anti-government or anti-war. They were also barred from publishing any of their own writings.

Items supplied included a bed with mattress, sheets, blankets and a pillow. Many had their own money so were able to provide extra linen if they required it. They were also given a small wooden table and stool.

Many of the COs wanted to make their room a more comfortable and welcoming place to live in, so some hung curtains at their windows, even though these were still barred. Some hung pictures on their walls and in all respects attempted to make it their own homely space.

On the other hand, there were those who neglected even basic hygiene and some rooms needed a thorough clean. Dr Battiscombe, referring to an inspection he carried out on 5 Hall on July 5, 1917, wrote:

"Many cells were not really clean and one or two were extremely dirty. The bedding in one case extremely so."

Inside a cell

The directive with regard to care of individual rooms gave the following instructions:

"Cells should be scrubbed out once a week and brushed out daily. Bicycles should not be permitted in the cells." (Medical Journal 23 May, 1917 entry made by Deputy Medical Officer, G Hillyer)

Two days earlier, Dr Hillyer had written when inspecting 2 Hall:

"Sheets and pillow cases should be changed more frequently, many being in a very dirty condition."

It was an individual's responsibility to take dirty linen off his bed and take it to the laundry where he would collect clean sheets and pillow cases with which to remake it. Facilities were provided to enable individuals to keep their room and bed clean, but the responsibility was entirely their own. One inspection report by Dr Battiscombe on December 12, 1917 noted:

"A large number of the cells everywhere are excessively untidy owing to the large amounts of rubbish etc. stowed away under the beds and in corners. Many of the walls are covered with dust etc. of some standing and require brushing down."

However, even those who had made the effort to care for their own room came in for some criticism of their living conditions in the same report:

"A certain number of the cells were found with curtains drawn over the windows—this is inadvisable as the deodorising effect of daylight and sunlight is not obtained. Cells were stuffy, odorous and stale. There is very little ventilation and little fresh air as the doors being closed. This should be remedied."

An indication of the dampness of the interior of the work centre arises with the requirement that bedding needed to be aired daily. 4 Hall in particular was identified as that with the highest level of damp. Bedding was to be aired on the rails of landings. However, this caused hygiene concerns because:

"When the bedding is taken in at midday, the dinners below are liable to be contaminated." (Dr Battiscombe Journal entry, May 17, 1917)

But he goes on to say:

"The bedding *must* be aired, but the rails in 4 Hall do not appear to be the best place for that purpose."

Blankets airing on the rails

No alternative arrangement was ever documented in the medical journal but presumably a solution was found.

Inside the Wider Walls

Dartmoor Prison had been built to accommodate up to 1200 convicts, and the cells were arranged in cell blocks up to five stories high. In addition, there were domestic areas and also those for administration, work, recreation and punishment. There was also a chapel and a library.

The Prison Library with well-known photographer W Tetley on the left

Although the basic layout could not be altered when its change of purpose to a work centre was announced, some areas were closed off to the COs whilst also allowing for greater freedom with no door locks and additional areas for recreational activities. Facilities now included a reading room, common room, concert room and a gymnasium.

One of the main areas closed to them was the church inside the prison on the orders of the Bishop of Exeter. Mark Hayler, who was a CO at the time, was quoted as saying:

"The Bishop of Exeter refused the conscientious objectors the use of the church in the prison. If we'd been murderers, we'd have had a free hand and could have sung 'God save the King'." (IWM Sound Archives 357/28)

Within each room there was no running water or toilet, as you would expect to find today. For general personal washing and shaving, they could collect hot water from a central supply to take back to their room. Access to the bath house was freely available to all, but facilities would have presented some limitations and lack of privacy for over 1000 men. Designated taps supplying fresh drinking water were available and the men were advised by Dr Battiscombe not to drink water from outside sources as it could be polluted.

With regards to toilet facilities, there were outside earth closets which were to be used during the day. There were two toilets on each hall landing only to be used as an emergency at night after lights out. This could present some problems. One of the Conscientious Objectors, for example, was identified as having a sexually transmitted disease (STD). The other men were concerned about sharing toilet facilities with him and he was allocated one outside earth closet near to his room in 2 Hall for his use only. It would be cleaned by the sanitary party, but he was himself held responsible for the 'sitting bar' being kept clean.

The other consequence of his condition meant that concerns were also expressed as to whether his laundry should be mixed with theirs. Laundry was done centrally for all COs, but following the raising of this matter, he was allocated a time during the week to do his own washing.

Meals were cooked in the kitchen by men designated as kitchen staff. Conditions were unsatisfactory from a health and hygiene point of view as was clearly indicated by Dr Battiscombe following one of his regular inspections:

"The kitchen was crowded with men; some working, others standing and sitting about, waiting for their dinners, I presume. The odour of humanity was much in existence!" (Medical Officer Journal July 5, 1917)

A further inspection on September 17 caused him to write in his journal:

"I considered it to be in an unnecessarily dirty state. In particular the rims of the coppers had not been scraped clean—the scrapers were dirty with dried foodstuffs; the scrubbing brushes for coppers were dirty and lying in dirty water. Greasy knives, sticky jam tins etc. were lying all over the place. The pipes and ledges had accidentally not been cleaned for some time!"

Many COs complained about the quality of the food served to them. Various issues revolved around the freshness and quality of the food delivered to the work centre as well as the way it was presented. Some examples of this included inedible vegetables, particularly potatoes damaged by frost, margarine that was often rancid, fish of poor quality and unfit for consumption and cooking fat with an unpleasant odour which tainted the food and could not be used. This led to more

Conscientious Objectors buying their food from other sources.

Dr Battiscombe, as ever, took an unsympathetic view of the complaints and on September 9, 1918, he wrote:

"As regards the quality, any complaint on this score is frivolous: the food is as a whole much superior to that obtainable by the poorer members of the general public."

He had previously offered a recipe for a nourishing soup using the rations provided. The recipe read:

"One pint of soup consists of 6ozs of uncooked meat, 4ozs uncooked lentils or beans and 2ozs of uncooked vegetables. This of course would make a solid meal, but the men refused to eat the beans, and they wish to have more fresh vegetables in lieu." (MO's Journal, July 20, 1917).

Those working in the kitchens did not necessarily have previous experience, so it is no wonder that food was:

"Badly cooked, greasy and burnt." (MO Journal, October 8, 1917)

Whatever the quality of the meals on offer, the quantity was favourably remarked on by Eric Dott (CO):

"The food is in abundance and we have all meals together."

Tables laid for a meal in a cell block

Another CO, Alfred Downs, would have disputed this as he noted on 28 July, 1917 that he was: "Very much in wanting of food." He used his freedom of movement and his own money to buy a loaf and margarine.

A special effort was made for Christmas 1917 and it is recorded in the story of William Ralph Done, a CO at Princetown at the time. A 600lb pig was slaughtered providing the meat, and although it consisted mainly of fat, this gave flavour to the meal along with potatoes and turnip. A Spotted Dick sufficed as a Christmas Pudding and in all it provided a welcome highlight to Christmas for the men.

Conscientious Objectors' Committee

A small committee of elected COs organised and ran many aspects of daily life inside the work centre within the parameters set down by the Home Office.

Although the work centre was a more relaxed environment than the previous prison regime, this did not mean that there was a lack of discipline and punishment for infringement of the rules.

Therefore, the manager, in cases of discipline decided the outcome; the responsibility for ensuring that the right person was punished fell upon the committee. In one case, a CO returning from the village refused to give his name to the gatekeeper. The manager requested a member of the committee to identify the man in question, but he refused to do so. This raised a question in the House of Commons on Monday, May 7, 1917 as to the wisdom of allowing these committees to continue in their role. The response from Mr W Brace was:

"It is much regretted that the member of the men's committee would not induce the offender to give his name, but I cannot say that he was under any obligation to do so. The committees elected by the men serve a useful purpose, and I do not think it would be desirable to do away with them." (COs' Hansard, May 17, 1917).

One of these 'useful purposes' was to instigate various recreational social clubs and activities. As previously mentioned, facilities inside the work centre gave opportunities for reading using the well-stocked library and a reading room, meeting and socialising in the common room or exercising in the gymnasium. The concert room was put to good use not only for those whose interest was music but also for the drama group. These groups organised and performed plays and concerts for presentation to the other men. Programmes were produced for these events using the print room which was part of the old prison facilities. The works presented by the drama group were often serious undertakings, one example being *The Great Adventure* by Arnold Bennett, performed on two evenings in December 1917. Even when they were about to be released from Dartmoor Work Centre, they put together a farewell concert: "The Last Appearance in this Settlement of all Old Favourites."

Advertisement of the farewell concert

A lot of the men were being redeployed and leaving the settlement, even though the War had not ended. The Farewell Performance programme is dated 1 July, 1918.

There may have been further drama and concert performances after this date, but they would not have been on such a scale as these productions.

Programme schedule

Other leisure activities on offer included a debating society, religious group meetings, football and other sports. In addition, during their leisure time the COs were permitted to leave the centre for cycling, walks on the moor, visits into the village of Princetown and as far afield as Plymouth initially. As the prison chapel had been closed to them, COs who wished to attend religious services had to visit the local Methodist chapels or go to the Friend's Meeting House in the village.

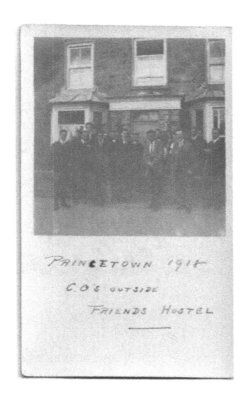

C.O's outside Friends Hostel, Princetown 1918

The COs' committee would be called upon by the men to mediate in cases of dispute between their members, or to convey grievances or complaints to the manager and staff. Primarily their role was to ensure that all members' rights were protected and to ensure that life was as bearable and as comfortable as possible for all.

Some members of their community may have preferred not to visit 'Bolt's', the local village shop, but wished to buy extras if funds were available. The committee set up and organised the running of their own shop within the work centre. This supplied mainly consumable goods, including tinned foods, biscuits, cakes, margarine, cocoa, loose nuts etc.

Settlement community shop, 1917

As Mr W Brace indicated, the committee played a very useful role within the work centre serving the interests of the men whilst also providing a useful point of liaison with the manager and staff.

Discipline

As noted elsewhere, COs were subject to disciplinary procedures and sanctions. These would not, of course, include corporal punishment as with the previous inmates of the prison. The work centre inhabitants would not suffer floggings or birchings and had already witnessed the closing off of the chain room. Neither would they have their diet restricted as a punishment as in previous times when errant prisoners had their rations reduced to bread and water.

The basic rules covered work and work times, curfew times and a general code of acceptable behaviour both inside and out. Contravening the set codes would incur some form of punishment from minor to severe.

The severest measure was for the CO to be recalled to the army or sent back to prison. Rule 16 laid down by the CECO (Committee of Employment for Conscientious Objectors) states:

"Public propaganda whether by making speeches, taking part in processions or demonstrations, or otherwise, is forbidden."

Conscientious Objector D A King fell foul of this rule. He was returned to the army after writing a letter to the CECO stating that he refused to obey the rule which forbids propaganda by men released for employment under the committee's rules. Sir George Cave (Home Secretary) in reply to a question raised in Parliament replied:

"As obedience to the rules of the Committee was one of the conditions on which he was released and excused from military service, the Committee had no choice but to recommend to the Army Council to recall him to his unit." (COs' Hansard No 39, August 2, 1917)

William Durston, another CO, was recalled from Princetown to the Army but subsequently sentenced to two years imprisonment for an offence committed after his recall.

Breaking Rule 16 was not the sole reason for recall to the army or a prison sentence, as in the case of Alfred Catherall, who was recalled to the army from the work centre. Following an injury sustained whilst working, he failed to return to work after his allocated sick leave. He gave the explanation that he had been 'visiting a friend'. As his previous work record had been less than satisfactory, this final misdemeanour earned him the recommendation from the War Office that he be recalled to his unit.

A further example of a CO being recalled to military service was as a result of a shooting. A more detailed account of this will be dealt with in a later section.

Monetary fines could be imposed to varying degrees. COs were paid 8d per day with a 1d deduction a day for National Insurance. This was in line with the 1½d per day that soldiers paid out of their 1/0d (5p) per day pay. It was considered fair that as a CO's pay was 2/3rds of that of a soldier, their insurance contribution should be in the same ratio. A further deduction of up to a maximum of 6d per day was made in cases where a separation allowance was paid to the man's family. An allowance of 1/7d (8p) a day was paid to any man who was absent from his quarters for a complete day upon the committee's approval. This could be either working away or on official leave. Fines were usually made for arriving late for work at 1d for every occasion.

Privileges could be withdrawn. One that affected all those at Dartmoor Work Centre was the ban on visits to Plymouth and neighbouring villages and towns. This followed incidents with members of the public and service men on leave.

Although confinement to quarters was not a frequent punishment, on one occasion this sanction was invoked for all COs. On the death of a fellow CO, Harry Firth in February 1918, all the men went on strike for a day in order to escort his coffin to the local railway station. All were subsequently confined to their quarters after work by the Manager, Major Reade, for 14 days. Also, the two ringleaders who were responsible for calling the strike were sent to prison. One of these was C H Norman. Leading up to this event he had been a consistent offender against the legislation regarding the spread of anti-war propaganda. He frequently attended meetings forbidden to COs making public speeches at them. He had escaped the ultimate sanction for these infringements of Rule 16, but inciting the strike resulted in him finally being sent to prison for two years hard labour along with the other instigator, J P Hughes.

The Funeral Cortege of Harry Firth

When questioned in Parliament about the consequences to the COs for not adhering to the rules and the punishments meted out, Mr W Brace answered:

"Of the men sent to Princetown by the CECO, nine have been sent back to prison or recalled to the army; 15 have been awarded by the committee various punishments from the stoppage of six weeks' pay downwards; and up to the 5th instant, 62 punishments have been imposed by the manager under the summary powers conferred on him by No 33 of the rules recently laid on the Table." (COs' Hansard No 30, May 24, 1917)

Medical Provision

The medical officer (MO) at this time was Dr Eric Battiscombe, highly recommended for this role. He joined the prison service in 1907 following many years of general experience. He was transferred to Dartmoor as Deputy MO in 1911, before becoming MO when his predecessor Dr S Dyer left. During this period Dr Battiscombe was assisted by Dr G Hillyer and Dr S Craig.

Battiscombe kept a comprehensive journal which informs clearly many aspects of daily life within the work centre. Some of his comments have been quoted already in previous sections. His journal shows that his responsibilities included far more than dealing with the sick or injured. His role included the overseeing of living conditions in respect of hygiene in individual rooms and halls, quality and quantity of food, hygiene and safety in the kitchens and outside hazardous working practices. He was also in charge of sanitation, not only with regard to the toilet and washing facilities but also ensuring the whole drainage system inside the centre walls was working efficiently.

His medical duties included the care, not only of the COs, but also of the work centre staff and their families.

His medical abilities encompassed a wider range than would normally be expected today. He performed simple dental operations and extractions amongst the staff and their families. Due to a Home Office ruling regarding the use of anaesthetics, the COs elected to see either one of their own men or a practice outside the centre.

Dr Battiscombe performed minor surgical operations in the Work Centre Hospital, but for more serious cases he was able to call upon the skills of a local surgeon. He also had the responsibility for optical and dental care. However, the COs had the choice of going elsewhere for treatment if they preferred.

He ran a daily clinic for the casual sick who would report to him outside of their working hours for treatment. The men were not afforded the same privacy as today. Although consulted individually, this did not take place in a separate room from others who would be waiting. There were occasions for privacy, however, when the consultation was of a particularly serious or sensitive matter.

Exterior of Prison Hospital

Interior of Prison Hospital

Perceiving the medical officer as merely concerned with sickness and injury in his role at the work centre is to completely understate his responsibilities. In Dr Battiscombe's own words from an entry in his journal dated 3 August, 1917 and headed 'Complaining Sick', he testifies:

"These numbers are certainly somewhat large, but they do not comprise sick applications only."

The phrase 'Complaining Sick' includes any and every application to the medical officer; waste, clothing, leave, transfer, health, broken spectacles, enquiries regarding friends, food, in fact everything.

"Amongst the sick applications are included trivialities, for which no man would dream of seeing a doctor, but would attend to in his own home, such as abrasions, slight cuts and sprains, constipation and the reverse, colds etc.

"Here, in the settlement, the men must apply to the hospital as they have no means of procuring anything themselves. In some cases, it is necessary to give a man two or three doses of medicine in a day (out of labour hours) in cases of acute diarrhoea, cold etc. Each repeat dose is written down and this helps to swell the numbers.

"It must not be forgotten that all these various applications are made out of labour hours.

"In all big communities, there are always a few unnecessary sick applications made by a certain class of men, but they are very difficult to detect, and in the long run it is cheaper or more profitable to give a few extra doses of 'Black Draught' and keep the men quiet and contented than to waste reams of paper and envelopes and hours of labour in refuting charges of 'lack of medical attention etc.'

"Again, the majority of these men have never been accustomed to hard physical outdoor labour, and this in conjunction with the altitude and the climate of Dartmoor, together with lack of skill in handling tools helps to swell the numbers.

"Taking everything into consideration, I do not consider that the proportion of sick men is unusually large."

E Battiscombe, MO.

Add to this the need to examine and weigh all the newcomers who arrived with no medical records, his workload would be extremely demanding. At this time, of course, there was no National Health Service, so many men arrived in poor medical, dental and optical condition. It is to Dr Battiscombe's credit that all men, when leaving the work centre, took with them a comprehensive medical record.

Although Battiscombe was obviously conscientious in carrying out his duties towards the staff and their families, the COs and the health and hygiene considerations within the centre, he also felt an obligation towards safeguarding the public purse. He weighed the needs of the COs against his view of reasonable expenditure. Add to this his attitude towards the COs which reflected the overriding public opinion:

"It must not be forgotten that these men are abnormal." (MO's Journal, June 28, 1917), and his low opinion of the Conscientious Objectors:

"We have noticed however, that the class of men received here has much deteriorated and very few of them are suitable for what would be called 'real hard work' in civil life." (MO's Journal, August 31, 1917)

It is clear that the COs, in his opinion, had a limited claim on public resources. Evidence of this is seen where individuals may have been considered in need of treatment in Tavistock or further afield. Many dental or optical visits were only carried out at the individual's own expense. One CO was given permission to travel to Plymouth for the purpose of having his eyesight tested free by the optician, but he had to pay his own travel costs. Battiscombe later arranged with an optician in Tavistock to see and test any CO at a flat rate of 10/6d per visit:

"The question who pays I leave to the Home Office." (MO Journal, August 21, 1917).

Dental treatment was another area of medical need that incurred expense to individuals. There were amongst the COs, qualified dentists who would carry out some minor treatments for payment. However, emergency extractions were carried out by Dr Battiscombe at public expense. Having removed one man's carious teeth and noting that there were several other partially decayed teeth, Battiscombe said in the journal:

"As further treatment is not likely to endanger his health and efficiency, I do not recommend that the work should be carried out at the public expense." (MO Journal, August 20, 1918)

Dental treatment could be funded from the public purse in cases where poor dental health would impact on an individual's general well-being. When considering the matter of whether false teeth should be supplied to a CO by government funding, Battiscombe wrote:

"As his health is not likely to be seriously impaired for the want of them, I am not prepared to recommend that they should be supplied at the public expense." (MO Journal, May 7 1918)

He further remarked:

"That with the soft food now imminent his health will not necessarily suffer if he does not procure a new set at all." (MO Journal, May 20 1918)

Monetary considerations were not confined to just dental and optical treatments. Some medical conditions were also subject to individual payment by the CO. In one serious case, a man with rodent ulcers on the face needed to have a course of electrical treatment which could only be carried out in Plymouth or London. His travel to either city would be at his own expense, as would the treatment. Following his application for permission to travel, Battiscombe suggested that:

"If permission is granted, it should be forwarded here with little delay as the disease is a serious one." (MO Journal, May 23 1917)

It would be assumed that any injuries incurred whilst working would receive attention at no expense to individuals.

The same was not applied to injuries sustained during leisure time, as in the case of a CO who tripped over a stone whilst out walking. He dislocated his right elbow but could not be X-rayed at the time because it was so swollen. The CO could not afford the cost of the X-ray locally but would be able to do so if he was allowed home.

"I consider an X-ray examination to be necessary, but to save public expense I suggest he be granted a month's leave and told to arrange for the X-rays himself." (MO Journal, November 5, 1918)

Owing to the fact that this injury was done outside of working hours, apart from having to fund his treatment himself, all the time that he was absent from work was unpaid. His daily rations allowance of 1/7d was still payable.

Although the preceding accounts exhibit some of Battiscombe's professional, and some might say harsher, dealings with COs, he did show a compassionate side on occasion.

A CO who looked older than his years and showed symptoms of senility, was also observed as being unable to walk far or do any meaningful work. Battiscombe recommended him to be given an 'absolute release'.

"From the point of view of the army, he is quite useless and no board would pass him in any capacity." (MO Journal, August 20, 1918)

It is well known that at the end of the War, there was an outbreak of Spanish Flu which killed thousands of people worldwide. The work centre was not immune from this and many men became infected and were hospitalised (see Appendix), one of whom, Henry Haston, died. As he died whilst being detained at Princetown, a public enquiry was held on the 28 October, 1918 into his death. The coroner, Mr Brown, stated that he was perfectly satisfied and that everything possible had been done for the deceased. The cause of death was registered as Pneumonia arising from natural causes. This is all detailed in Dr Battiscombe's journal entry dated October 29, 1918 where he also stated that:

"Mrs Haston, sister-in-law, on behalf of herself and the widow, expressed satisfaction to the coroner, and also their gratitude to the CO brothers and sisters and to myself."

There was only one other death, during the time of the COs at Dartmoor Work Centre, which was completely unrelated to the flu epidemic. This was the death of Henry Firth, which led to the strike in February 1918 when the COs refused to work so that they could accompany his coffin to the station. This death raised questions in the House of Commons. These matters raised revolved around concerns as to whether Firth's death was as a result of his being in a physically unfit condition to carry out the work allocated to him.

On 9 February, 1918 the Western Daily Press published an article which reported on the findings of the inquest into his death. The reporter states in his article that,

"The deceased was of poor physique and was put on light work."

The nature of his work and workplace was raised by Mr King, MP in Parliament, on February 14, 1918. When referring to Firth's death, he stated that:

"When he went to Dartmoor he was in an enfeebled condition, but set to work in a quarry, punished for not working hard and only sent to hospital when past recovery."
(COs' Hansard No 58, February 21, 1918)

Sir George Cave, Home Secretary, replied that Firth was sent to Dartmoor at his own request and was passed as fit for labour by the medical officer at Maidstone Prison. He also stated that he was put on light work in the quarry and disputed the allegation that he was punished for not working hard.

The debate then centred around the diagnosis and treatment of Firth's diabetes. According to Sir George Cave, the symptoms of diabetes appeared after he had been working in the quarry and that he was then immediately admitted to the prison hospital. The Western Daily Press records that:

"A Dowlais, solicitor, representing the widow, and Mr C N Norman, representing the Men's Committee, put questions with the object of showing that the deceased was not treated properly."

This concern formed part of the debate in Parliament, not only in relation to his diabetes but also with reference to his physical condition and needs. Sir George Cave in response to a question raised by Mr Whitehouse, MP said:

"I believe that when the man said he was cold, the doctor replied that the men in the trenches were cold too."

In mitigation of Dr Battiscombe's comments to Firth he added:

"He (Dr Battiscombe) had no reason to believe that the man was unwell, and he treated him as a well man, except that he allowed him to wear his overcoat." (COs' Hansard No 58, February 21, 1918)

There is no doubt that the causes of Firth's death caused much concern amongst MPs in the House but also unrest amongst the men at the work centre. Answering a question raised by Mr King about the strike by the COs on or about the 6 February, Sir George Cave responded that:

"About half the Conscientious Objectors in the Dartmoor Work Centre refused to work on Friday last. They alleged as their grievance that one of their number, Harry Firth, who had recently died, had not been properly treated by the Medical Officer." (COs' Hansard No 58, February 21, 1918)

Summarising his faith in the professional abilities of the man, Sir George Cave in one of his comments said:

"Dr Battiscombe, the Chief Medical Officer at Dartmoor, is a man of high qualifications and long experience. I have his qualifications before me. He is a man upon whose record no one would hesitate to say that he is eminently qualified for an appointment of this kind." (COs' Hansard No 61, February 28, 1918)

A more unusual case that Dr Battiscombe had to deal with was the shooting incident mentioned previously. Although accidental, this incident resulted in questions being raised in the House of Commons, not so much in regard to the victim this time but as to the availability of a revolver to the COs, and whether the authorities had knowledge of it. Dr Battiscombe detailed the injuries as:

"The bullet perforated the right testicle and then entered the right thigh where it still remains. The injury is of course serious, but is unlikely to be dangerous to life." (MO's Journal, November 12, 1917)

As with all other cases which may require an operation, in this case the removal of the bullet, Battiscombe could either perform the surgery himself, or in more complicated presentations, call in the services of an outside surgeon. The decision in this instance was that he would perform the necessary operation without outside help.

Other cases included one of sunburn of the thighs from 'sunbathing naked', rheumatism and arthritis, ear infections, heart conditions and general illnesses, all expected to be dealt with on a day to day basis.

Injuries and accidents were common at work and were part of the routine cases seen by Dr Battiscombe. Some were fairly minor whereas others were more serious. These will be dealt with later.

It would not be unexpected that another facet of health that the MO would need to deal with would be mental illness and wellbeing. Before detailing some of the cases of mental issues and Dr Battiscombe's remarks, it must be remembered that the context in which these took place was vastly different to the attitudes of the modern day. Soldiers at the front exhibiting signs of, what we now acknowledge to be, PTSD were not subject to medical help and under these circumstances there would be no sympathy for COs who were not facing the terrors of War.

Dr Battiscombe had no more sympathy for the COs than a vast majority of the general public would have. In his Journal, Battiscombe writes of one such CO who he described as 'neurotic', and who persistently worried about his wife and children and the effect that air-raids would have upon them.

"The mere fact of his coming here as a CO disposes of any anxiety as to their safety; otherwise he would have joined up and helped to try and prevent them (air-raids)." (MO Journal, October 5, 1917)

One CO's mental state was assessed by Dr Battiscombe in his Journal of 26 June, 1917:

"Mentally he is a crank and a spiritualist, and the borderline between sanity and real convictions and insanity with hallucinations or delusions is very vague."

Battiscombe considers that no further steps need to be taken, but in response to the obvious misplacement or theft of the man's clothing, advised him to:

"Use his alleged spiritualistic detection powers for the consideration of the mystery of his clothes and the detection of the criminals."

A non-violent man was reported to be hospitalised for observation by Eric S Craig, a deputy medical officer, on 2 November 1917. He assessed no immediate 'causes for anxiety'. On November 12, Battiscombe, having returned from leave, observed that:

"His condition has not improved and, in my opinion, is unlikely to do so in his present surroundings."

He agreed with the previous assessment that the man was: "Not violent, but is difficult to control, and it has been found necessary to retain the services of another CO in the settlement to look after him continuously. I recommend that he be sent to his friends for an indefinite period."

After application to the Home Office, permission was granted for the CO to go home into the care of his adopted father.

"There is no necessity to certify him as insane." (MO Journal, November 26, 1917)

Battiscombe affirms the cause of the CO's mental state as rooted in religion. He summarised that the man was:

"Naturally somewhat weak-willed and emotionally religious, he came under the attention of some of the CO fanatics. As the only Israelite in the settlement, he was unable to stand his ground: his ideas became chaotic and he finally broke down."

He somewhat recovered after a fortnight in the hospital, but then on returning to the general community:

"The fanatics were too persistent, and two weeks later, he had to be readmitted. By this time, he had lost all his beliefs and was in a state of blasphemous excitement."

Finally, Battiscombe, noting that there was no sign of this mental disturbance on the man's arrival in June, wrote:

"Removal from the settlement influences to his own home surroundings will probably clear up his mental condition in a comparatively short time." (MO Journal, November 26, 1917)

In Battiscombe's journal, he has made reference to 17 cases of men who had some form of mental illness. He obviously considered that some of these men would benefit from light work away from the main community. He recommended that they be employed in the Medical Officer's Light Gardening Party under the supervision of an officer. He observed the benefit of this, remarking on one Conscientious Objector:

"A considerable mental improvement has taken place in the above. I consider the discipline here has been most beneficial to him." (MO's Journal, July 24, 1917)

Work

Conscientious Objectors had been offered work under civilian control in lieu of military service which they had accepted, and came to Dartmoor Work Centre, Princetown, under those conditions.

Roland Reigne (CO) considered that:

"The work was in no way of a military nature, so that there was nothing to which one could really object. There was the usual internal work such as making mailbags and employment in the laundry, kitchen, stores, cleaning and maintenance etc. Outside the walls, others worked at the Prison Gas Works, and the 2,000 acres of land attached to the prison provided employment for the majority. Some worked in the garden and farm parties, some with reclamation parties and others in the quarry."

The perception of the COs having an easy life at the work centre, who were labelled by the Daily Mail as the 'Dartmoor Do Nothings', was not altogether accurate. Long working hours in an often climatically hostile environment, work place injuries and the testimony of many of the COs to their working conditions, disputes this claim.

Roland Reigne comments:

"All the work was carried out in the traditional penal system of labour; that of doing it the hardest and most laborious way. Generally, the plant and tools were of heavy make and with the intention of producing fatigue."

In return for their 8d pay per day, COs were allocated various employment. Consideration was given to their previous experience, skills and physical abilities, and a judgement made as to whether they should be given lighter duties or whether they were capable of much heavier work. This was not always successful in every aspect, as W H Payne, a CO, a small man of 5 feet 3 inches with a slight physique shows. Struggling to throw earth up from the bottom of a five-feet-deep trench, Battiscombe recommended:

"That he be utilised for surface work in the same party, or be transferred to a party where the depth is not more than, say 2½ feet." (MO's Journal, July 6, 1917)

Additionally, concern was expressed by Roland Reigne, who acknowledged that all the COs represented practically all trades and professions. Many men were unsuitable for hard, laborious work and he notes that:

"Doctors, in particular, must have been very concerned about their hands."

Of the total number of COs employed at the work centre, approximately 200 were allocated work within the centre walls. These jobs were to ensure the day to day efficient running of the facility. These would include work in the laundry and kitchen, although, as previously noted, the kitchen staff were not particularly conscientious with regard to hygiene and food presentation, and on the whole had no previous catering experience of providing for over 1000 men.

The kitchen staff did not only comprise of cooks, but also dishwashers and servers.

The jobs of the kitchen staff were not necessarily secure if their work was not satisfactory. Responding to complaints over the hospital diets, referring to the food as badly cooked, greasy and burnt and the dirty state of the tins and dishes containing it, Battiscombe wrote:

"These complaints I condone, and I suggest that a change of staff be advisable. I refer to that position of the kitchen staff that have anything to do with the hospital diets—dishwashers, cooks, servers etc." (MO's Journal, October 8, 1917)

The laundry workers would have been responsible for the COs' cleaning and pressing of bedding, clothing etc. The picture of the COs' laundry party taken in June 1917 gives an indication of how the washing process was carried out. The CO on the far left appears to be carrying the piece of equipment used to agitate the articles to be washed in the large barrel of soapy water. Although indoor work, not exposed to the vagaries of the ever-changing Dartmoor climate, it would nevertheless be quite rigorous labour when doing the laundry for over 1000 men.

The Laundry Party

These occupations along with maintenance work and cleaning tasks may have been seen as 'lighter duties' in comparison with the tasks undertaken by those working outside the centre walls.

Repairing the Prison Walls

As well as the arduous nature of the outdoor work in an inhospitable climate for the greater part of the year, the validity of it as 'Work of National Importance' did come under scrutiny. Questions were raised in the House of Commons with regard to both the type of work and whether some of it was in fact pointless.

In answer to this, Sir George Cave affirmed:

"The work is, for the most part, agricultural, and if efficiently carried out, is of national importance. Most of the men still at Dartmoor are working satisfactorily."

Questioning the buildings of roads, 'which are of no consequence whatsoever', Sir C Kinloch-Cooke received assurance from the Home Secretary that:

"Most of the work is not road making, but agricultural work, reclamation of land and cultivation. Those who are making roads are presumably making roads which are of use."

Sir Kinloch-Cooke expressed his doubts by responding quite simply:

"No, sir." (COs' Hansard No 45, November 8, 1917)

One such road is locally known as 'Conchies Road'. This can still be walked along today and is nicknamed 'The Road to Nowhere'. It was envisioned as opening up the moor to accommodate two new farms linking them to Ashburton. By the time the COs were freed, the road was less than 2½ miles long. I took part in a BBC programme *Walks of Life* in 2019 where I took the presenter along this road explaining its origins.

It should be noted that Princetown's founder, Sir Thomas Tyrwhitt, in 1784, had leased a large area of moor from the Duchy. His aim was to drain and cultivate this land and form a community. His lack of success due to the climate led him to abandon this project and negotiate with the military and the government for the building of a prison to accommodate French prisoners of war.

Tyrwhitt's experience with horticulture would indicate that this aspect of farming 100 years later was unlikely to be appreciably more productive. The low yield of produce would not necessarily justify it as 'Work of National Importance'. This view was re-iterated by William Done CO who noted that:

"1917–18 was very wet in Devon and the land was very difficult to cultivate. Seed was sown in spring 1918 and there was poor germination and slow growth. When it came to harvest, there was hardly enough yield from the grain to equal the seed initially sown."

Add to this the way the COs were put to work, and it would cast more doubt on this as expressed by Mark Hayler CO:

"The agricultural work was absolutely penal and organised in lines as for convicts… Of course, the object was to make work. The harder it was and the more tiring it was, the better. Let me give you a few examples: there was a hand roller to which eight men were harnessed, engaged in rolling a field. I have been one of those human horses. The work we did could have been done by one man and a horse in a third of the time, and this, mind you in a time of the country's food crisis."

Agricultural Party

He was not the only one who expressed this view. James Butcher wrote:

"My party had to do a lot of grass mowing, and as some of them had never used a scythe, and there were plenty of rocks just peeping out of the ground but covered with grass, several scythes soon went west. Much of the work we did could have been done by the horses as they had grass cutters on the place, but it was done on purpose to find us a job."

However, those working on Tor Royal Farm, owned by the Prince of Wales, were on a section of the moor that had been improved but was in a bad state. COs with farming backgrounds and those with experience of horses were selected to work there. Ploughing the moor, sowing and harvesting were the responsibilities of the stable party. The ploughing work was carried out with ploughs each pulled by two horses, and with granite just below the surface, the damage to the ploughs was high. Eventually, the boulders were blasted with explosives to make the work easier.

Apart from land reclamation and arable farming, care of animals was an important part of the work. Hay was needed for animal food and was produced by hard manual work. James Butcher observed:

"I have seen over a hundred men in ten acres of hay, some with rakes, others with forks, and others shaking hay with their hands, and some of these fields of hay were all carried to the stacks with forks! How is that for Old England?"

The Milking Party

Animal husbandry was a legacy from the convict prison, as explained by James Butcher:

"There were cows, pigs, horses, and flocks of sheep, which had been looked after by the convicts, but now the COs had to carry on this work."

Boundary walls needed to be built and maintained for agricultural purposes. The method of building one such boundary wall was described by James Butcher. It was:

"…made with squares of turf, cut about 18 inches square; the wall would be four feet wide and six feet high, and must have cost as much to build as any brick wall."

Farm walls were not the only walls needing maintenance. The main construction material for building the prison and the village was granite. Most of this was produced in the prison quarry, known as Holme Quarry. Men were employed—blasting, stone breaking and carting the materials to various sites within Princetown. One such site was the 'Road to Nowhere' where stone was carted for its construction.

The Quarry Party

There is no doubt from the various opinions and writings of some COs that most forms of employment at Dartmoor Work Centre were laborious, the equipment provided was not designed for ease and efficiency for carrying out the work and the men were used in a 'penal' way. Mark Hayler, CO, gives another example of this:

"...All spades, shovels, barrows etc. were prodigiously heavy, weighted with lead probably. Everything was out of date to make the job more irksome. All the coke for the gas works and furnaces was carted by hand, teams of ten men being harnessed to a cart: ..."

The weather on Dartmoor was commented on by James Butcher who spoke of the fogs which could be so thick that visibility was reduced to a few yards. In addition, he speaks of the heavy rain which could bring the men in off the moor to work on different tasks. Eric Dott, CO, writes of one such arduous occupation, which they occasionally tried to lighten:

"Stone breaking is the task for wet days, though it needs to be pouring before we are kept in from Mis Tor."

He goes on to talk of the uncomfortable nature of working within the stone sheds which were open with only a roof, a back and two ends. Describing the work of breaking stones inside these sheds, he says:

"All this time you are cramped for room, the wooden plank you sit on is too near the stone bench and there are men crushed up against you on either side. You are very cold and desperately fed up. The men play draughts with the stones or keep a book beneath the bench to read at convenient intervals."

Inside the Stone Sheds

Any respite from the daily work routine was welcomed by some COs. William Done commenting:

"Many of the COs were put to work trying to maintain the prison blocks built to house French prisoners in the early 1800s. The chance to unload building materials from freight wagons was considered a pleasant relief from floor cleaning and laundry work."

Donald Grant, CO, found the benefits of transferring from an outside occupation to working inside the work centre in a more privileged environment. The moor not only offered no shelter from the winds and rain but was also much exposed in sunny weather.

"I first worked in the Agricultural group: hot weather, very tiring. However, I was offered a job as an orderly in the hospital after a fortnight. I then had a cell to myself in hospital and could have a bath at any time."

While not all types of work were necessarily equal in terms of hardship and purpose, their attitude to employment was summarised in a statement issued by the COs at Princetown in which they affirmed their willingness to work, but protested against the penal nature of it and demanded that it be work of real importance.

Work Accidents and Injuries

It can be seen from the COs own accounts that the vast majority of them were engaged in many types of extremely physically demanding tasks, and it is therefore not surprising that accidents and injuries were fairly frequent occurrences.

These were not always necessarily of a serious nature, and remembering Battiscombe's earlier words with regards to the men having no access to simple first aid equipment, he further notes that some of the accidents are:

"Most trivial and only require a slight dressing." (MOJ, May 17 1917)

There were, however, more serious accidents causing major injuries. The most serious of these was recorded by Dr Battiscombe, and in a letter to the wife of the injured CO, he wrote:

"I regret to inform you that your husband has just met with a rather painful accident, having been run over by a cart across the body. Whilst leading the dustcart, the horse became restless, knocked the man over, and in falling, the wheel ran over his abdomen just below the level of the umbilicus." (MOJ, May 7 1918)

In a further letter, he says:

"He has evidently suffered no serious internal injury." (MOJ, May 29 1918)

Two days later he goes on to say that the CO is progressing favourably but will have to remain on his back for another 3–4 weeks or possibly longer. The CO was hospitalised from May 7 to July 1, 1918. On his discharge from the hospital, he was deemed unfit for manual labour for some considerable time to come.

The majority of these men had no previous experience of working with animals and therefore accidents happened. One CO, Lewis Plummer, was in hospital for 12 days—the result of a kick by a colt on his shin, whilst William Watson was hospitalised after being thrown from a pony and hitting himself against a wall, damaging his arm and leg.

Horses were not the only animals that caused injuries. W H Bell stayed in hospital for 24 days after suffering ligament damage to his right knee, caused by a vigorous sheep which he was trying to catch.

Several men suffered hernias from heavy lifting and digging, whilst the quarry work accounted for crushed fingers, strained backs and similar types of injuries associated with heavy work of this kind.

Even farm workers working in the fields were not immune from accidents. Forks in feet, arms and even in the head are all recorded.

Roland Reigne's concerns about delicate hands were borne out by the case of Henry Worgan, who damaged his fingers. It is unclear how this injury occurred but according to Battiscombe:

"His occupation of pianoforte playing will be permanently impaired by a minor degree only." (MOJ, April 5, 1918)

The only death which could possibly be argued as work related was that of Henry Firth whose death has been dealt with earlier. Many men who worked at Dartmoor left for other centres and prisons etc., so it is not clear how many casualties died from work-related illnesses. One CO, Paul Leo Gillian, was transferred to Winchester Prison from the work centre and died a few weeks later possibly from suffering from the hard regime incurred at Dartmoor.

Life Outside the Walls

By the time the COs arrived at Princetown, several men from the village had already lost their lives fighting in the War. There could be no doubt that the families whose men folk had been enlisted would bear resentment towards the COs arriving at Dartmoor Work Centre. The attitudes of the majority of the general public towards them had already been felt by these men following their declarations and exemption since 1916. As part of a hate campaign, many of them had received a white feather, the symbol of cowardice. Verbal abuse was common, and in some cases, actual physical violence was meted out to them. Prior to the opening of Dartmoor Work Centre, there was a large protest meeting in Plymouth, campaigning against bringing the COs to Devon. Within Princetown itself, once the local population was aware that they would be definitely arriving and hearing of the freedoms they would be allowed, strong feelings surfaced. James Butcher, CO, noted that:

"When they first heard that the COs were coming to their prison, and would be allowed to buy food etc. in Princetown, a meeting was held, and most of the shopkeepers and bakers decided not to sell them bread etc."

A typical anti-Conscientious Objectors postcard

One of the shopkeepers, Albert Bolt, who ran a general store, was the only one to go against this tide of feeling and was willing to sell to the COs in his shop. James Butcher, CO, continued:

"One man stood apart from the rest, and sold to anyone who wished to buy; needless to say that with 1000 men in the place, it soon made his business a very flourishing one indeed, and when the others awoke to this fact, they tried to claim some of these customers, but a good many kept to the man who first served them."

Bad feeling wasn't confined to the shopkeepers as the villagers were seen to suffer shortages due to the buying power of the Conscientious Objectors. Sir C Kinloch-Cooke, in a speech in the House of Commons on 30 April, 1917, said of the COs:

"They eat up nearly all the food in Princetown and the neighbouring towns. They clear the shops and take all the sweets that people usually buy for their children." (COs' Hansard No 27, May 3, 1917)

He went on to say that:

"They crowd the shops, and they purchase the best of everything that the town can provide."

In the previous section, with regard to the rations provided, it is evident that these were seen as adequate. The local people were now seeing that in addition to these rations, these men could spend their own money in the local shops depriving the village population of many goods. They not only had the means to buy, but some were also receiving food parcels and a good deal of correspondence from their families which led to Sir Kinloch-Cooke to further comment in the House of Commons:

"They have a collection of food sent to them in parcels and, would the House believe it, it takes four men to drag a hand barrow every day with the postal deliveries." (COs' Hansard No 27, May 3, 1917)

He was an MP who took a harsher view of the way that the COs should be treated and questioned their freedoms. This was not a view of all in the House of Commons, one of whom, Mr Joseph King, raised concerns over the treatment of

Conscientious Objectors. In a previous debate it was stated that none of the discipline methods used for convicts were applied to COs. He disputes this in the case of food rations. He refers to a report by the Prison Commissioners dated March 31, 1917 about the treatment of COs. He read just one sentence of the report which was:

"Dietary restriction is the principal instrument of punishment."

He questioned the starving of men who were expected to do hard work.

"This is just the policy that has been habitually and deliberately adopted by the Home Office towards the people of Dartmoor. They were admitted, even by the War Office, to be genuine and engaged on work of National Importance. That being so they should be decently treated." (COs' Hansard No 45, November 8, 1917)

This was certainly not the view of all MPs in the House who proposed that COs should have no food or post sent to them and that they should not be allowed to buy food.

Conflicting attitudes towards the COs were also evident amongst the work centre staff and management. James Butcher writes regretfully of one warder who forged good relationships with some of the men in his charge:

"I remember a friend from Yorkshire and myself were invited by one of the warders to supper, and of course we went, and had a fine time. I am sorry to say that this man got along so well with his party that the authorities saw fit to change him to a lower form of work in the gas works, and as he refused to take the job, he was dismissed from the service after being a warder for 16 years, and nearing his pension. He was one of the few who had anything of the man left in him and dared to show it; the others were machines running without any oil."

Needless to say, these men were not unfamiliar with verbal or even physical abuse when they ventured outside of the prison walls. Many of the population still harboured resentment against them, and this hostility was shown by some throughout the duration of the war and beyond. Even though they were a common sight in and around the village, some would never accept their presence at Dartmoor Work Centre without demonstrating their virtual hatred towards them. This could not be considered surprising given the circumstances described by Sir C Kinloch-Cooke, who listed amongst the grievances against the COs:

"They wander about Princetown and the neighbourhood of Dartmoor talking to young people, most of whom have fathers or brothers or uncles who are fighting at the front."

He continues, "These men congregate at the street corners and wait for the opportunity when people are coming out of the shops."

Their purpose in doing this was to put their points of view, even denigrating the King. Some even requested that the work centre warders changed the buttons on their uniforms as they bore the insignia of a crown. Sir C Kinlock-Cooke also reported an incident where a group of COs physically attacked a police sergeant at Princetown. The antagonistic feelings aroused by these men and the actions of some were typified by Sir C Kinloch-Cooke's comment on a recent photograph published in the Daily Mail of COs in Princetown:

"Look at the countenances of these men, their grinning faces, looking like apes!" (COs' Hansard No 28, May 10, 1917)

Animosity being shown towards a CO outside the church in Princetown

This photograph, reportedly taken by a passing boy at the time, shows the depth of feeling of one local lady towards a CO being allowed to 'freely' walk the streets, by hitting him with her rolled umbrella.

Most of the COs were undeterred by these types of encounters and continued to visit the shops and other facilities within the village and further afield. For some, train travel being restricted to twice a year, walking into Tavistock, a round trip of 14 or so miles, or even to Plymouth, some 28 miles return, would be the activity of choice for an afternoon or a whole-day leisure trip. Some, however, preferred not to run the gauntlet of local anger and chose to use the shop set up by the COs committee within the work centre.

Contact with the village residents could not always be avoided, even by those who preferred to steer clear of confrontation. Those who worked on the open moor or at local farms would have to encounter these villagers to and from their place of work.

The railway station was at the opposite end of the village to the work centre, and for those travelling home for leave, the train was their only means of transport. This was, however, limited and their entitlement to leave and train travel was explained by Mr W Brace in the House of Commons on 19 April, 1917:

"The regulations formerly provided for one working day leave per month, but they now allow four days leave after three months, and another six days after 12 months, in addition to the usual public holidays." (COs' Hansard No 27, May 3, 1917)

This was another cause for concern as, on December 6, 1916, all soldiers had had their leave suspended, and yet these men, just four months later, were given leave to go away at Easter. Not only that but some of them had had their train fare paid.

Mr W Brace put the facts before the House stating:

"Of the 856 Conscientious Objectors at the Princetown Work Centre, 274 were allowed to go on leave at Easter, and of these 166 had their fares paid." (COs' Hansard No 27)

Following this the HOCECO ruled that the leave of COs employed under them would be suspended except in exceptional circumstances. Mr W Brace, on April 27, 1917, went on to say with regard to the movements of the men of Princetown:

"The Committee has decided that they shall not be allowed to visit towns and villages outside Princetown." (COs' Hansard No 27)

Venturing onto the moors on foot or by bike was a leisure time activity enjoyed by many of them. James Butcher described how:

"We finished work at dinner time on Saturdays, then we could spend the afternoon on the moors, and often had picnics; we were allowed a radius of a few miles around."

Conscientious Objectors enjoying a picnic on the moor

In Sir C Kinloch-Cooke's view, this privilege was abused by some who used this freedom for propaganda purposes:

"They get four hours in which to roam about the country every evening to spread these pernicious doctrines. Of course, they have Saturday afternoon and Sunday thrown in. Dartmoor is a very favourite resort for a large number of people in that part of the country. This year the mothers will take their children there whist their fathers and brothers are fighting at the front. Are these men to be allowed to accost them and to press on their children their pernicious doctrines?" (COs' Hansard No 28, May 10, 1917)

He further questioned in the same speech the Conscientious Objector's use of a local facility intended for warders' sons:

"The Warders' boys cricket ground is commandeered. Why should they have a ground to play on? They go about in batches and annoy people."

An important aspect of many COs' lives was their faith encompassing a wide range of religious beliefs. Roland Reigne, CO, summarised this diversity:

"Most Christian denominations, from Roman Catholic to Quaker were represented, and also a few other faiths. And quite a number of Agnostics and Atheists."

Although there were religious group meetings organised within the work centre by the men themselves, it must be remembered that the Bishop of Exeter had ordered the closure of the Prison Chapel. Those, therefore, who wanted to take part in a chapel service were able to attend those within the village. One such place was:

"A Wesleyan Methodist Chapel that was well attended and several COs became Methodist Ministers." (William Done, CO)

One attendee was CO James Butcher who described his own experience:

"I used to attend a Wesleyan Chapel in Princetown on Sundays; in fact the place was almost run by COs, so many men had gone to the war—there were one or two warders who were members of the Chapel, and the Prison Chaplain sometimes attended because when the convicts went, he had little to do; the COs could supply scores of local preachers, also some young ministers."

Chapel attendance by the COs was seen in a different light by Sir C Kinloch-Cooke who saw them as using the chapel as another opportunity to show their protest and antagonism towards the King and Country and the war currently being fought.

"These men were taken to church in the neighbourhood, and when the national anthem was sung, they got up and went out. Prayers to our soldiers and sailors are omitted from the service." (COs' Hansard No 28, May 10, 1917)

Mr W Brace, in answer to this, had made inquiries of the Wesleyan Chapel Minister. He avowed that he had seen no evidence of objection by the COs when the national anthem was sung and that prayers for soldiers and sailors and others in authority were said.

This was later contradicted by the minister himself when further inquiries were made following an assertion that at divine service, the singing of the national anthem saw six men leave, and others remained sitting whilst the rest of the congregation stood. Mr W Brace informed the House:

"The Wesleyan Minister informs me he saw no one leave during the singing of the national anthem on 29 April, but he believes that several sat down."

(COs' Hansard No 29, May 17, 1917)

Sir C Kinloch-Cooke found the COs' further involvement in chapel life questionable, and he said:

"Some of the men are actually allowed to teach in the Chapel School. I consider it to be an outrage that these men should be allowed to teach their views to children. They must not allow these Conscientious Objectors to teach in schools, whether in chapel schools, or church schools, or any schools whatsoever." (COs' Hansard No 28, May 10, 1917)

DIVINE SERVICE

EVERY SUNDAY AFTERNOON

IN THE CHAPEL

Commencing at 3 o'Clock

CONDUCTED BY THE CHAPLAIN

FREQUENT ADDRESSES BY MEN IN THE SETTLEMENT

You are cordially invited.   HYMN BOOKS PROVIDED

Invitation card to divine service in the chapel

The hostility of many of the villagers didn't make allowances even for those attending religious services. Joseph Hoare, CO, wrote:

"I remember some of the COs from Princetown going up to the Church for a service and being stoned on the way. The parson was standing on a flat tomb stone; I won't say cheering them on, but at any rate encouraging them."

Even villagers themselves who were seen to make friendships with COs were subjected to similar treatments. Percy Leonard, a CO, wrote:

"A (Quaker) family invited me to spend an evening with them in their home. After that I spent quite a few evenings with them. Once there was a riot outside the house and the mob threatened to burn it down because they had COs inside. We were about six or seven there, and they packed us down in the cellar."

Although the attitudes of a few local residents show an acceptance of the COs at Princetown, it was certainly not the case with the majority.

Some COs were fortunate enough to be able to move their families from their hometowns to rented accommodation within the village. Alfred Downs, CO, in his notes made whilst at Dartmoor Work Centre, expressed great concern about his family, especially as his wife was expecting the imminent arrival of their baby. His additional concern was noted on October 2, 1917 when he wrote:

"Much concern over air raids. Wanting Ada and children to come to Dartmoor."

He talks of:

"Looking for a place for Ada and children to come down. Not easy. Agreed to share a cottage with Mr and Mrs H. 10/- per week all found except sheets, blankets and pillows. Ada arranged to forward these."

The move took place in March 1918 which must have been a cause for great comfort for Alfred Downs and his family.

Visits from family members were allowed on occasion. However, the distance many would have to travel to this remote location was somewhat prohibitive.

Two Conscientious Objectors with their wives outside the prison gates

If they did make the journey, many were able to stay locally, and accommodation could be found at the Friend's House or at private homes occupied by sympathetic villagers.

Alfred Downs received many visitors. He wrote:

"Feeling much better now at Dartmoor. Mrs Salter has been to see me, also Mrs Smith. Also, Florrie and Jack. Jack not in the Army."

Religion was not the only driving force for COs. Political beliefs, as already indicated, had a large part to play in the lives of many.

Roland Reigne wrote:

"Politically, there may have been a few conservatives, certainly liberals, most were socialists and some of more extreme views such as communists etc. With so large a company holding such differing beliefs and opinions, and with so many being ready to air their views, it amounted to almost a 'Babel'. With the exception of a few who were prepared to fight under certain circumstance such as a war against capitalism, we were united and held in common a 'Conscientious Objection' to all war."

As already seen, attendance at religious meetings was not confined to inside the work centre, and according to Sir C Kinloch-Cooke, neither was attendance at political meetings. He inquired of the Home Secretary:

"On whose authority the Conscientious Objectors at Princetown have been allowed to hire a cottage for use as a kind of club; whether this hostel, as the Conscientious Objectors call it, is a hotbed of revolutionary propaganda, and will he cause inquiries to be made with a view to the closing down of this establishment?"

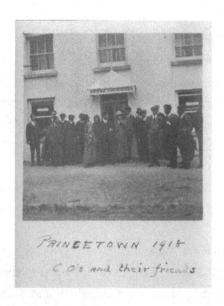

Princetown 1918, C.Os and their friends

Mr W Brace replied:

"I understand that a building in Princetown called 'The Friends' Hostel' is rented by a committee of the Society of Friends, and is open to Conscientious Objectors while out on leave. No meetings of any political organisation have been held on the premises, and no literature, other than books or magazines of general interest, is sold or distributed. A meeting for worship is held every Sunday evening. At present I see no ground for interference."

(COs' Hansard No 57, February 14, 1918)

Much of the evidence has pointed to the diversity of opinion with regard to the convictions and actions of the COs. Many people believed, as the above question from Sir Clement Kinloch-Cooke indicated, that these men were politically motivated and not only showed their anti-war feelings but also demonstrated an apathy towards the King and the country.

Others showed a certain understanding and respect for their views and expected them to be treated accordingly.

The antagonistic feelings of the majority of the Princetown residents were probably representative of those of the general public, but would have perhaps been felt more deeply as they were daily reminded of their presence in their village.

An interesting anecdote, noted by Alfred Downs, shows that in some cases, even those who had lost loved ones in the conflict, could take a softer view. He wrote in December 1917:

"Borrowed a cycle to go round the prison. A horsewoman caught me up and wanted to know of conditions in Dartmoor. She said she was impressed. Went along the road for a mile together. She had lost her all beloved and would have preferred to have known him to have been in DCP instead of dead."

Aftermath

The end of the War on November 11, 1918 did not signal the immediate closure of Dartmoor Work Centre, nor indeed the immediate freedom of the Dartmoor Conscientious Objectors.

There were several reasons for this delay in allowing these men to return to their homes and normal way of life. One main consideration was that although not viewed as 'prisoners', they had none the less been 'sentenced' to a certain length of detainment in a prison or at a work centre. Many of them had been originally sent to prison for defying military orders. These release dates were to be adhered to.

In addition there was the question as to whether these men should be released before all military personnel had been repatriated and enabled to return to their homes and families. A question was raised in the House of Commons by Sir Clement Kinloch-Cooke, MP:

"Is the prime minister aware that some of the persons who evaded military service by taking advantage of the conscientious objection clause in the Military Service Acts and were ordered to do work of national importance have been set free, and will he consider the advisability of issuing such regulations as will prevent any further release of these men taking place until the last man serving in the navy or army, under the Military Service Acts, has been demobilised?"

(COs' Hansard No 86, February 27, 1919)

The question of returning to a normal way of life would include the ability to work. COs' own writings described the variety of trades and professions that these men had been engaged in before the war. It was now considered that the returning soldiers and sailors should be given priority in the search for employment and the COs were not allowed to seek work near their home. The account of William Ralph Done, CO, a farm worker before the war, states that:

"With the armistice in November 1918, the system was relaxed. I was allowed to return home to live but not to work... This restriction continued into mid 1919 when I finally returned home to work."

Notwithstanding these restrictions, COs found it very hard to secure employment. Attitudes of many were still set firmly against them and their refusal to fight, and prospective employers were not exempt from this general feeling. Some COs found that after a successful application and subsequent call to interview, they would receive a rejection when answering the question, "What did you do in the war?"

In May 1918, James Skelton, CO, had been given permission to apply for employment, and wrote to his previous employers where he had worked as a print designer before the war. The reply, written by a director he had obviously known well, not only stated that through lack of orders due to the War, no position was available, but also offered him some personal advice:

"Now, for heaven's sake, set yourself right with the rest of humanity; throw over the suave gentleman who lives in the clouds and come down to earth where there is hard work to do, and some of it, as all earthly work, is not always quite clean; otherwise there would be no earth on earth, but only heaven all round us. To that state, neither you nor I have been able to travel yet."

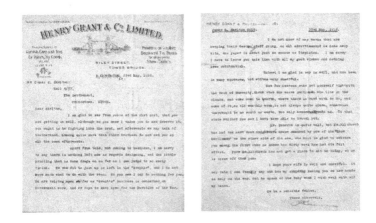

A letter from Heny Grant & Co Limited

He finishes with:

"I hope your wife is well and cheerful. At any rate I can frankly say she has my sympathy having you on her hands as well as the War." (Letter dated 23 May 1918, Henry Grant & Co Ltd, Riley Street, London)

This was not to be Skelton's only refusal. One of the most telling rejection letters was from Charles Pearson & Son of Mansell Street, London, who wrote on 5 July, 1918:

"In reply to your letter of yesterday's date, we might say that as we have conscientious objections to conscientious objectors, we cannot entertain your application."

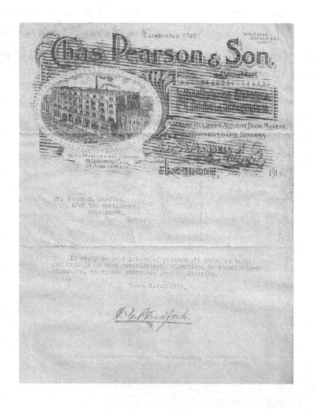

Letter from Charles Pearson & Son

It was not only the views of the employers themselves, but also their sensitivities towards other workers that encouraged them to reject his application for work.

"We have no desire to criticise the views you hold, but when it is considered that 87% of our skilled Operators have joined the Army, and having regard to the feeling of these operators, it is considered not advisable to engage the services of anyone holding views such as you give us to understand you hold, whether they be right or wrong." (Letter dated August 8, 1918 from Sergeant Brothers, Abergavenny)

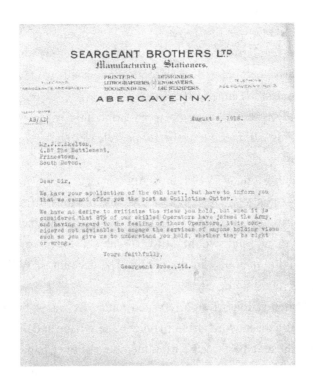

Letter from Seargeant Brothers Limited

Although these letters are all dated before the end of the War, it would be reasonable to assume that this was the type of reaction an application from a Conscientious Objector would evoke. Indeed, in some cases they were not even considered in the application process as the initial advertisement would state, "Conscientious Objectors need not apply."

Although life outside of the work centre would undoubtedly present many challenges to the COs, they would nevertheless be anxious to return to normal life at home with their families. Awaiting this release from Dartmoor Work Centre, a date was finally set.

The regular newsletter distributed to all its members by the Christadelphian Brotherhood announced to those at Dartmoor in the June 1919 edition:

"Before these lines appear in print, this camp will be closed, as all members are to be released before Easter Monday."

Easter Monday 1919 fell on April 21.

Conscientious Objectors would face obvious difficulties with providing for their families with the obstacles to employment, and would still be subject to abuse from unforgiving members of the public. The account of William Done's return home cites:

"After William Ralph returned home, he was subject to some ill-chosen words from people in the village and in some cases, those remarks came from members of the Chapel."

Another restriction placed upon them was that they were prohibited from voting for the next five years. The representation of the People's Bill of 1917 gave woman the right to vote but denied this right to COs.

As for the work centre, it reverted to its previous purpose as a convict prison. The type of convicts held were very different to the ones incarcerated there before the War.

In October 1919, the manager, Major Edward Reade, left Dartmoor for a post at Maidstone Prison and was replaced by Major T H Wisden. In 1920, the warders then became known as officers.

The 1916 Military Act was repealed in 1926 and the records of the COs were ordered to be destroyed. Fortunately, the COs' Hansard Records remain, as do some written evidence from the COs themselves, enabling some insight into their life at Dartmoor Work Centre.

From the COs' Hansard No 87 dated March 13, 1919, the cost of the scheme for the employment of Conscientious Objectors from August 1916 to December 31, 1918 was £254, 992/15/9d. (In 2020 value, this amounts to £13.5 million)

List of Conscientious Objectors known to have been at Dartmoor Work Centre, Princetown, March 1917 to April 1919. (taken from documents at Dartmoor Prison)

Total number known 1236

P W Barker October 2019

A - J	K - R	S – Z
ABBOTT George	KAY H	
ABRAHAMS Joseph	KAYE W H	SAMPSON A
ACKROYD E	KEELING H R	SAMUEL D
ACTON W	KEELING S	SANDERS Wilfred H
ADLER H	KEENE F	SANDERSON A B
AHLQUIST A F	KEMP E F	SANDFORD Arthur
AINSWORTH F	KENDALL A C	SARGENT H J
ALDERSON Thomas	KENDALL L C	SAUNDERS Percy D
ALLAN W M	KERR J	SAWYER A E
ALLEN L A	KERRIGAN G	SCHNEIDER R
ALLEN Reginald	KERSHAW H	SCOTT A C
ALLEN T	KEWLEY G	SCOTT Harold
ALLISON A	KEWLEY J	SCOTT J
ALLMAN J A	KEY I P	KEY I P
AMBROSE A E	KICK O	SEEHAM L
ANDERSON C G	KING D A	SELBY W A
ANDERSON E T	KING E C	SENIOR H
ANDERTON F	KING S J	SENIOR J
ANDERTON W	KING W L	SHAKESHAFT William
ANDREW W	KINSEY T J	SHARMAN J H
ANDREWS L A	KIRK L	SHARP Joseph A
ANTHONY E R	KISBERG S	SHAW C
APPLEBY D	KNIBBS W R	SHAW J G
APPLEYARD T	KNIGHT Thomas B	SHAW J L

ARMOUR A D	KNIGHT W H	SHEFFIELD J W
ARNOLD E A	KNIGHTS E W	SHERBURN J
ARNOTT J	KOOP Charles	SHERMAN J
ARTHUR E J	KOSTELLO F	SHIELDS J C
ASHBY Jed	KUHLS E H	SHUTE Montague A
ASHEL H W	KYLE J	SHUTTLEWORT H H F
ASHLEY Austen	LAMBERT T W	SIFFLEET P A
ASHLEY J	LAMPTER M	SIM A
ASHLEY H A	LATTER Alfred Edward	SIMKINS S
ASTILL J	LATTERY F R	SIMMONDS W J
ATHERTON A	LAW J	SIMPSON G
ATHERTON R	LAWRENCE R E	SIMPSON R H
ATKINS John W	LAWRENSON S	SIRRALL W J
ATKINSON W C	LAWSON Ernest	SKELLERN Clarence
AUTY C	LAYCOCK Ernest	SKELTON James S
AUTY E	LAZARUS A	SLATER A
BACON C W	LEAKIN F E	SLEEP P H
BAGALEG F W	LEATHLEY A	SLEITH W J
BAILEY A A	LECK C E E	SLOAN J
BAILEY A G	LEES N	SMITH A J
BAILEY Lewis	LEES W	SMITH A T
BAILEY Walter	LEFCOVITCH Harry	SMITH C P
BAKER H H	LESTER A V	SMITH Charles Taylor

BALDOCK Edward T	LESTER J M	SMITH George F
BALDOCK G	LEVY B	SMITH Horace H
BALDWIN H A	LEWES S T	SMITH J
BALDWIN James h	LEWIS Albert J	SMITH L
BALLINGER John	LEWIS C	SMITH N W
BAMFORD H	LEWIS D J	SMITH O W
BAMFORD J E	LEWIS E D	SMITH P
BAMFORD Percy	LEWIS F	SMITH P A
BANBURY Richard	LEWIS G	SMITH R C
BANKS A	LEWIS J	SMITH T J
BANKS Clifford	LEWIS P W	SMITH Vivian
BANKS Cyril	LEWIS R	SMITH W E
BANKS Dennis	LEWIS T	SMITH W J
BANKS Lewis	LEWIS W	SNOWDEN J
BANN Frederick	LEWIS W H C	SOLE William J
BANNISTER N	LEY Reginald Henry	SOUTHWELL H H
BARDLE W J	LIBOVITCH M A	SOUTHWELL J
BARDSLEY Albert	LIDDY Douglas	SOWLES A
BARKER L W H	LIGHTON Charles	SPALDING J A
BARKOWSKY Henry	LIGHTOWLER Gilbert	SPEDDING H
BARNES A C	LILLEY H	SPENCE K
BARNES Clarence E	LIPMAN J	SPLITT W E
BARRETT J T	LISTER C K	STANLEY J R
BASHAM J	LITTLE J F	STANTON W

BASTIN F H	LLEWELLYN A B	STANYON H
BATCHELOR J	LOCK W R	STARKEY
BATEMAN G	LOGAN J	STARLING E
BATEMAN G L	LOMAN A W	STATHAM Arthur J
BATHGATE H S	LOMAX A W	STEAD E
BATLEY Lewis	LOMAX H E	STEED W
BAXENDALE H	LONG E	STEEL J
BAXTER R H	LONGDEN Frederick W	STEEL M
BAYNES F A	LONGSON J E	STEEL W A
BEALE W J	LONGSTAFF P	STEPHENSON W
BEAR J	LOOK G F	STERN Mark
BEARD Frederick A	LORD W J	STETT A R
BEAUMONT E	LOUDEN T	STEVENS A
BEAVIS W D S	LOWDEN G	STEVENS E N
BECK M	LOWE Billy	STEVENS W
BEEVER Basil	LOWE H	STEVENSON A F
BEIGHTON F	LOWER A F	STEVENSON C F
BEIGHTON F C	LUDLAM E B	STEVENSON J
BELCHAM R H	LUFFMAN H	STEWARDSON A W
BELLCHAMBER A E	LUMAN H E	STEWARDSON R
BELL John Edgar	LYE F	STEWART G M
BELL W H	LYLE W	STEWART R
BENNETT R	MACAULAY N B	STODDART J

BENNISON J	MacDONALD L	STOKES Thomas
BENSON E A	MACDOWELL H M	STONE E W
BENSON F C	MACKAY D	STONE J G
BERKOV J	MACKAY F H	STONE Sidney P H
BERKOVSKY Henry	MACKIE F W	STONELY N
BERRY E V	MACKINTOSH John	STOTT D F
BEYNON H	MACREADY H	STUART C C
BICKARD W F	MADGWICK W G	STURMLEY J
BIGDEN A E	MAHONEY A G	SUCHETT J T
BIGDEN H C	MALLARD D K	SUTTON Arthur
BILLING H	MALLARD N	SYMONS H
BIRD W	MANN W P	SYMONS P O
BIRKBY Amos Arthur	MANTELL S G	TAIT J H
BISHOP George A	MARCHANT E	TANNER J W
BLACKBURN J L	MARKER B	TAPPER J P
BLACKMORE E	MARRIOT P	TEAL
BLACKSHAW S	MARSHALL A H	TEMPKE I
BLAKE Alexander	MARSHALL J	TEMPLE J
BLANCHARD O G	MARSHALL R K	TETLEY W
BLANCO C F	MARSON W S	THEOPHILUS D B
BLANDFORD J	MARTEN Howard	THOMAS B
BLANEY J B	MARTIN A E	THOMAS G

BLYTH A	MARTIN E A	THOMAS G V
BOAT F	MARTIN R A	THOMAS H
BOCKING George	MASON J C	THOMAS O
BODDY H E	MASON W L	THOMAS R C
BODEN J	MATHER H G	THOMAS Stafford H M
BOLE D B	MATTHEWS John	THOMAS T
BOLTON W H	MATTHEWS O J	THOMAS W C
BONNAUD V F G	MAUNSON E G	THOMAS W J
BONNER A H	MAY W	THOMPSON Edward
BONNER Bernard	MAYNE C S	THOMPSON Henry
BOOTH F	MAYNE E L	THOMPSON J
BOOTH Harry	McBRAIN A	THOMPSON M E
BOOTH J T	McCORMICK F	THOMPSON R E
BOOTHROYD B	McDONALD A	THOMSON G
BOWELL G M	McDONALD John	THORNE G T
BOWEN F	McDOUGALL A L	TIPPETT A H
BOWER H	McELLEN J C	TODD T
BOWERS W	McILVEN George	TOLL Alfred Norman
BOWKITT W R	McINNIS A	TOLL Edward Albert
BOWLES	McINTOSH Benjamin	McINTOSH Benjamin
BOWLES Arthur	McKAY D	McKAY D

BOWLES G M	McKIE J C	TONKS A C
BOWNESS H	McLEAN D	TONNER J
BOXALL W J L	McMILLEN A	TRACEY S T
BOYACK T A	McMURCHY W	TREGENZA C N
BOYD W A	McTAVISH D C	TREGENZON A
BRACEWELL Nimrod	MEACOCK W J	TREGENZON Chas Wilfd
BRADFORD W T	MEADOWS J	TRUSSWELL A
BRAILSFORD F	MEARES J	TUCKER H V
BRAIN T A	MELHUISH A G	TURNER H
BRAITHWAITE A	MELLOR Grieves	TURNER W H
BRAITHWAITE H	MELLOR W	TYSON D
BRAITHWAITE T A	MENCOCK W	UNTHANK W W
BRAMLEY T	MEREDITH H C	UNWIN A
BRAMLEY W E	MEYCKLES J	UNWIN H
BRICKLEY J	MILES H	UTTLEY W
BRIDGER Henry John	MILLARD S	VASS G J H
BRIERLEY J	MILLEN Ernest	VAUGHAN T G J
BRIGDEN H C	MILLER A H	VILES W T H
BRIGGS E	MILLER H J	VIPROID I W
BRIGGS Thomas	MILLER J W	VODEN W J
BRIGHTMAN Harold	MILLER William Fredk	WADDEN H T
BRIGHTON F	MILLS A	WADDLE W H
BRITTON W E	MILWARD H	WAITE L
BRODIE G	MINNS N G	WALDEN E G

BRONNARD V F G	MINSKULL C	WALDEN T A
BROOK H	MINTO J P	WALKER A W
BROOK Norman	MITCHELL C	WALKER E A
BROOKER W A H	MITCHELL E H	WALL Iram G
BROOKES E E	MITCHELL F N	WALSH John
BROOKES H	MITCHELL F W	WALTER M
BROOKS Frederick J	MITCHELL H C	WALTERS C H
BROOKS J	MITCHUM W	WALTON Maurice
BROOKS M	MOLEY J	WAPLINGTON J
BROOMFIELD S	MONNSEY F	WARD F
BROTHERTON J E	MONTGOMERIE	WARD N A
BROWN Archibald	MOODY G D	WARR G H
BROWN	MOORE F P	WARR R
BROWN G	MOORHOUSE Ernest	WATKINS T
BROWN H J	MOORHOUSE W	WATSON S
BROWN J H	MORGAN J	WATSON William
BROWN O	MORGAN W	WEARE P C
BROWN R W	MORRIS A J	WEBB E
BROWN T	MORRIS Isaac	WEBBER D H
BROWN T C	MORRIS William	WEBBER G H
BROWN W F	MORRISON W B	WEEKS A H
BUCKLEY H	MORRISSEY F	WEIR J
BUDD C E	MORTON J	WELLS R W

BUDD G	MOSCOVITCH L M	WELSH J
BULL H	MOUNTFORD	WEST R
BULLARD G	MOYER G A	WHARISKEY J
BULLARD H	MUIR A	WHARTON Lambert W
BULLAUGH A	MULKAHY C E	WHATTON T
BULLER George	MUNRO D M	WHEATON A
BULLOCK J	MUNRO Richard	WHEELDON Ince
BULLOUGH H	MURFITT F W	WHEELER A W
BUNTON P R	MURRAY J	WHELDON H
BURWELL W	MURRAY S C	WHITE A
BURNISTON A L	MUTCH J S	WHITE T
BURNS A	MUTCH T W	WHITE W H
BURROWS A	MYERSON A L	WHITEHEAD F
BURROWS J N	MYERSON S	WHITELL H
BUSH A L	NATHAN Samuel	WHITEMAN D C
BUSH T	NAUMANN Ludwig	WHITEMAN H
BUSHLEY H	NEAL J W	WHITFIELD Frank M
BUSSELL D	NEWBURY A C	WHITFIELD H D
BUSSELL R E	NEWTON A M	WHITTAKER T
BUTCHER C G	NICHOL J	WHITTE W
BUTCHER James	NICHOLAS R J	WHYBREW Walter
BUTT G B	NORMAN Clarence Hy	WIGGINS A L
BUTTER T	NORRIS R	WIGGINS R L & H

BUTTLE Walter	NORTON A	WILCOX E S
BUTTLE C G	NOTELLO F	WILLIAMS A J
BYNON H	NOUILLES J	WILLIAMS D J
BYRON E	NUNN Ernie	WILLIAMS E R
CAMPBELL A W	NUNN George	WILLIAMS F M
CAMPBELL George	O'DALY P	WILLIAMS J C
CAMPBELL J	OFFELL Henry Bernard	WILLIAMS S H
CAMPBELL S	ORR W	WILLIAMSON A
CAMPLUTT A W	ORRELL E	WILLIAMSON E
CANDLIN R D	OSBORNE A	WILLIAMSON F
CANE E	OSBORNE Frank A	WILLIAMSON H
CANNELL G	OTLEY K	WILLIAMSON M
CANNELL S J	OTLEY Mark Collins	WILLIAMSON O
CARMAN T H	OUGH N G	WILLIAMSON T
CARNEJIA O L	OULD Herman L	WILLIS Stanley W
CARR H S	OUTTEN Frederick	WILLOUGHBY T J
CARSON Thomas	OVERBAY E	WILSON A P
CARSON W	OVEREND Wilfred	WILSON P
CARTER P C	PAGE F	WILSON W
CARTER W T	PAGE J S	WILTSHIRE F
CARTON Peter	PALMER C C	WILTSHIRE H
CARTWRIGHT R H	PALMER S	WILTSHIRE H
CARTWRIGHT Wallis	PARISH P	WINTLE W L
CARVER H H	PARKER A M	WISHURST E

CASTLE J	PARKER L G	WITTMAR W
CATHERALL Alfred	PARKES A	WITTMER W
CHADBURN Frederick	PARKINSON J	WOOD Cyril
CHADWICK J	PATTERSON E M	WOOD J B
CHANDLER George	PAYNE F H	WOOD W
CHAPMAN Charles W H	PAYNE H	WOODALL P
CHAPMAN H	PAYNE W H	WOODMARCH A H
CHAPMAN J	PEACE P	WOODRUFF F
CHARING BULL W H	PEARCE F	WOODWARD E
CHARLESWORT H Alfred	PEARCE M G	WOODWARDS L
CHARLESWORT H E	PEARSON G H	WOOLAND G H
CHARLESWORT H W	PEDLAR W J	WORGAN Harry
CHIDGEY A G	PENDLEBURY J H	WRAGG C L
CHRIMES A G	PERRY A T	WRIGHT G
CHRIMES H	PETCH R	WRIGHT H D
CHRISTOPH R D B	PETERS W R	WRIGHT W E
CLARK J	PHILBY Samuel	YILES W
CLARKE C	PHILIPS C A	YOUNG S R
CLARKE E J	PHILIPS C J	ZACKHEIM S
CLARKE F E	PHILLIPS A	
CLARKE J H	PHILLIPS Harry	
CLARKE James	PHOENIX J	

CLATWORTHY Alfred E	PICKERSGILL Mark R
CLAY A	PICKUP J H
CLAY H	PILLING J
CLAYTON E	PINCH H S
CLAYTON E L	PINCH J
CLAYTON G P	PINDER D H
CLAYTON H	PINKERTON P A
CLEOBURY W T	PITTS A B
CLYMA Fredk Plimsoll	PLANK C
COBURN W S	PLATT J
COGGINS M E	PLATT T
COHEN C	PLATTEN W H
COHEN H	PLAYER E S
COHEN S	PLUMMER Lewis H
COLE Ernest T	PLUMMER S W
COLEMAN George Henry	POLLARD
COLLARD H	POLLARD B
COLLINS Joseph H	POND Ronald E
COLLINS M	POND W J
COLLINS S W	POOLE F W S
COLLINS T J	POOLE Sidney
COLLINS W	POSTEN A H
CONEYBEARE R	POWELL D R
CONIN W	PRATT R
COOK A E	PRECIOUS H
COOK J	PRISCOTT C
COOKE J S	PRICE H
COOPER Ernest W	PRICE T
COOPER F G	PRIESTLEY Walter

COOPER Samuel	PRING J
COPELAND R	PRITCHETT J
COPPLESTONE H	PRYOR F
COPPLESTONE L	PUGH R E
COPPURCH George	PUGMIRE H
CORDELL A E	PUGMIRE P
CORKHILL George S	PUGMIRE S
CORNISH W G	PULLINGER F
CORT E	PURVES N
COTTAGE W S	QUARMBY E V
COUCH D	QUICK J
COUPES T	RABIN L
COUPLAND F	RAINGE B P
COUSTON Robert	RATTER M
CRACKNELL H J	RAWLINGS V W
CRACKNELL R	RAYNER A P
CRACKNELL William	RECORD C
CRADDOCK G	RECORD F C
CRASSWELL W S	REDWOOD C C
CREE J R	REED F
CREED S G	REES TL
CROCKER Bertie	REES W R
CRODEY E H	REID G
CROSS W A	REINGE Roland Joseph
CUILLES B	REINGE Sidney G
CUMBERLAND W	RENDLE T
CUMMING A	RENNIE W

CURRIE S	REYNOLDS J W
CURTIS T H	RHODES C H
CUTTING G	RHODES W
DANDO G	RICE E
DANIELL A L	RICE T
DANIELS A	RICHARDSON George
DANSER G	RICKETTS O G
DARBY R E	RIDGE J W
DARLING J	RIDGEWAY E
DARWOOD Cecil	RIDING H M
DARWOOD W A	RIDLEY D
DAVEY T G	RIPLEY P
DAVEY W E	ROBERT A
DAVID J	ROBERTS B
DAVIES E T	ROBERTS G B
DAVIES G H	ROBERTS L A
DAVIES J	ROBERTS O
DAVIES R C	ROBERTSON J
DAVIES T	ROBERTSON W B
DAVIES T G	ROBINSON T
DAVIES W M	ROGERS T
DAVIS A	ROOKSBY Arthur
DAVIS Cyril	ROSENBERG H
DAVIS H	ROSS C
DAVIS J H	ROSS W
DAVIS L	RUSSELL D N G
DAVISON Ernest	RUTHERFORD J
DAVY H P	RYCROFT H E
DAWSON Ernest	RYDER G H G
DAWSON H R	RYMAN John William
DAWSON J P	

DAWSON R C
DEAN Fred
DEANES J
DEARMOUTH J C
DELLER Lawrence
DEMMERY Ernest
DENNIS Hedley C
DENNY Percy
DESKIN A K
DEWHIRST
DICKINSON Harry
DICKINSON J E
DICKINSON S
DICKSON W D
DILTHEY Henry
DINSDALE E
DISLEY H
DIXON Arnold E
DODDY H E
DONE William Ralph
DONLEY J
DONNELLY Arthur C
DONNELLY J T
DOTT Eric
DOWDEN C H
DOWDEN J
DOWKES George
DOWNS Alfred
DREWER Sidney P
DRINKWATER B John

DUFF W M
DUNBAR J
DUNCAN J L
DUNCAN W
DURBRIDGE E W
DURHAM R E
DURSTON Edward
DURSTON William G
DUTTON W
DYER J W
DYKE
EAGLE P C
EASOUGH R
EBBING L
ECCLES W
EDDIE George B
EDKINS W
EDWARDS E O
EDWARDS F Ernest
EDWARDS O
EDWARDS W
ELAM L
ELDING L
ELLIS Ernest
ELLIS Joe
ENGLAND A G
EPSTEIN Elias M
EVANS B
EVANS J A
FARMER Henry C F
FARMER R A
FARRAR E H
FIERS John
FIRTH Harry

FISHER E A
FISHER H C
FLEGG P J
FLEGG Percy J
FLEMING A R
FLETCHER A E
FLETCHER A J
FLETCHER C F
FLETCHER J E
FLETCHER V W
FLETT G
FLOWERS F
FLYNN R C
FOGDEN J W
FORD J C
FORD P G
FORD W
FORSYTH J
FOSTER C H M
FOSTER E
FOX C B
FOY Mark Henry
FRADIN M
FRANCIS A
FRASER Donald G
FREAKES J
FRENCH S
FRETMAN H A
FREW J
FRIDAY A S
FRIDAY M
FRITH R
FRYER C H
FRYERS R H
FULLER A
FULLER R G
FUNNELL J
FURNISTON J

GABBOTT Cecil Parr
GADSBY R
GAHAGAN J
GARDNER B A
GELTICUS E
GEORGE C E
GERRARD John
GIBBONS H G
GIBSON J W
GIFFORD R J
GILBERT W
GILCHRIST W
GILLIAN Paul Leo
GILMORE Frederick
GLOVER
GODDARD F
GOLDEN W H
GOODFELLOW A G
GOODLIFFE W E F
GORDON B
GRAHAM F
GRANT C H
GRANT Donald
GRASIE J
GRAVES H
GRAVES J
GRAY A
GRAY C A
GRAY T
GREAVES H
GREEN A
GREEN H J
GREENHALGH Harold R

GREENWOOD R
GREGORY G B
GREGORY T W
GREIG James
GRIFFEN W
GRIFFITHS A E
GRIFFITHS Daniel F
GRIFFITHS Ralph P
GRINDALL J H
GRINDALL R
GROVES Arthur
GROWCOCK Frank T
GRYER F
GUEST Cyril
GURNEY A W
GURNEY E W
GUTTERIDGE A
GUY A
GUY M R
GUY W
GWYNNE
HADIN G
HAGG T L
HAINES T P
HAINSWORTH
HALL J C
HALL Stanley
HALLWORTH Herbert
HALTON C C
HALTON J N
HAMILTON T
HAMMOND J
HAMMOND William
HAMPTON H W

HANCOCKS W E
HANNINGTON J
HANSEN G E
HANSON E
HANWORT H B
HARDY G J
HARDY Herbert
HARLEY W
HARPER Francis
HARRINGTON E A
HARRINGTON J
HARRIS D O
HARRIS E H
HARRIS F P
HARRISON A C H
HARRISON Herbert
HART J
HARTLEY F
HARTLEY G
HARVEY S J
HARWORTH R B
HASLAM F
HASSELL A E
HASTON Henry
HATTON F W
HATTON R
HATTON W H
HAWKINS A J
HAY A
HAYE E
HAYER A
HAYES A E
HAYES M
HAYES S
HAYLER Mark
HEDGE Albert

HEFFORD George
HELLIWELL R A
HERSEY J C
HICK O
HICKMAN J E
HIGGINS A
HIGGINS H
HILL Archer N
HILL G
HILL J E
HILL Joseph G
HILLS Charles H
HINDMOOR W
HINKSMAN Hubert A
HINTON A C
HINTON Jonathan
HIRST A
HIRST J
HISBEN P
HOARE John
HOARE Joseph
HOBART A V
HOBART C A
HOCKADAY Harold
HOCKLEY Ernest
HODGKINSON C
HOER J B
HOFFMAN Max
HOGARTH Hugh
HOLDEN Donald
HOLDEN R
HOLDISH White
HOLLAND John
HOLMES A
HOLMES Harold

HOLMES W E
HOOKER Ernest C
HOPKINS C G
HOPKINS H
HOPKINS J J
HOPKINS R
HOPKINS W
HORNE R G
HOUGH F W
HOUSDEN J N
HOWARD George
HOWELL W
HOWSON J
HUDSON B A
HUDSON H
HUDSON J W
HUGGINS A
HUGHES D
HUGHES Emrys T
HUGHES J P
HUGHES W Y
HULL Bertram
HUMPHREYS C
HUNT S
HUNTER J
HURWORTH Robert
HUTCHEON J
HUTCHINGS C E
HUTCHINSON R
HYAMS Isodore
INGRAM A
INGRAM F E
INGRAM W J
IRONS R

ISAAC Albert Henry
JACKSON J M
JAMES Douglas
JAMES T
JARBIE F P
JARVIS John
JARVIS Walter
JEFFERY N J
JENKINS D
JENKINS F V
JENKINS H J
JENKINS L
JENKINS W J
JOHNCOCK E G
JOHNSON E
JOHNSON L C
JOHNSTONE S
JONES A E
JONES B
JONES F
JONES H A
JONES H J
JONES H S
JONES J M
JONES J T
JONES L
JONES P J
JONES W
JONES W A
JONES W L
JONES W T
JOULIE F P
JULLIAN F G

Officers at Princetown Work Centre 1917-1919

George Heppell   J R Simpson   Charles   Pratt   A Waters (Civil Guard)

Tyreman (Head of Works)   Endacott   (Foreman   of Works) N Brooks

George Henry Lewis (Farm Labourer)   J Worth (Gasman) F Worth (Gasman)

I Worth (Store Labourer)

Bacon   Pearce (Locksmith)   Gilbert (Messenger) Dawes

G R Williams   W Rundle   Green   (Stores Labourer) J Plant

Heggadon (Farm Labourer) F Heggadon W Worth   E G Cole S Cole   George   Cyril   French   George   Henry Halfyard James Carr (Chief Warder)

Chapman (Stores Labourer)   Hutchinson   Kellow   R Giles

Weekes   E J Duckham   Rupert   John   Coombs   J Blandford

Frederick Hutchins Frank Yudi

Preece (Stores Labourer) Eric Battiscombe (Medical Officer)

George Hillyer (Deputy Medical Officer) Eric S Craig (Relief Medical Officer)

Major E R Reade (Manager)

J R Simpson, Kellow and J Blandford were all principal warders whilst the others were warders or assistant warders

Influenza sufferers from 8/7/1918 to 13/4/1919

8/7/1918 A F Stevenson 11/8/1918 N A Ward 29/8/1918 H D Whitfield 9/9/1918 W Andrew 16/10/1918 H Haston (died) W J Lord 19/10/1918 J Berkov21/10/1918 J B Hoer F Monnsey T J Willoughby W Hopkins A Norton 22/10/1918 F P Harris R K Marshall H Dawson H S Pinch E A Walker 23/10/1918 R Fuller 24/10/1918 H E Boddy G Moody I Morris H Wiltshire B P Reinze 25/10/1918 J G Shaw S P Drewer A A Bailey R H Cartwright M Hayes M G Pearce E Long J L Blackburn 26/10/1918 W J Bardle C A Gray 27/10/1918 K Otley 28/10/1918 M Ratter 29/10/1918 W K Peters H R Keeling H E Lomax L Elding J H Pendlebury 30/10/1918 E Cane H J Sargent R Norris J Snowden 31/10/1918 T Williamson G M Bowles J L Duncan A F Lower E R Anthony E N Stevens E A Martin 1/11/1918 A B Pitts T Hamilton 3/11/1918 J C Hall 11/11/1918 E Long W J Smith T Allen 12/11/1918 J Cook 14/11/1918 J Meyckle 16/11/1918 H C F Farmer 18/11/1918 C Priscott W H Platten 19/11/1918 G B Butt 20/11/1918 N Mallard 21/11/1918 A Marshall J B Blaney 22/11/1918 G B Robert W Harley 23/11/1918 J Brierley 24/11/1918 A Osborne G Danser 25/11/1918 W Orr F W Hough 26/11/1918 N J Jeffery I P Key

V W Fletcher 27/11/1918 H Disley 28/11/1918 A Guttridge H G Gibbons A Brown J Whitell 29/11/1918 H Whiteman P Wilson D H Webber B Levy 30/11/1918 W P Mann W Andrew H Price 1/12/1918 M A Libovitch A Lazarus E Orrell 2/12/1918 J H Clarke N B Macaulay 4/12/1918 H Baxendale 5/12/1918 R C Smith W Viles J Chadwick 6/12/1918 J Kerr 7/12/1918 J Southwell 8/12/1918 R Irons 11/12/1918 A Unwin F Kostello 12/12/1918 W Ross 14/12/1918 A T Smith J P Minto 15/12/1918 F Keene

23/2/1919 A Hassell 7/3/1919 F Jones 20/3/1919 E Auty 22/3/1919 C F Fletcher 24/3/1919 I Lipman 25/3/1919 E O Edwards 27/3/1919 T W Gregory 28/3/1919 F W Mitchell T C Brown 31/3/1919 W Rennie J Sherburn J Quick W J Lord L Moscovitch

G Flett A L Myerson E T Davies 2/4/1919 T Thomas R Atherton

S G Tomlinson 3/4/1919 S Mantell G Bateman H Wheldon

A E Griffiths 5/4/1919 R Belsham 7/4/1919 H Buckley G M Stewart 9/4/1919 L Copleston 10/4/1919 J Graves 11/4/1919 F Booth

M G Pearce 13/4/1919 E Orrell

All the influenza patients were discharged by 18/4/1919.

The last recorded date for a discharge was for 28/4/1919 for T G J Vaughan who had undergone an operation for appendicitis on 4/4/1919.

The first patients to be admitted to the hospital were T Platt, S Simkins and D M Munro on 14/3/1917

Bibliography

DELL, Simon *(2017) The Dartmoor Conchies,* Dartmoor Company.

ENSWORTH, Jones (2008) *Will We Will Not Fight,* Aurum.

KRAMER, Ann (2014) *Conchies – CO's of 1st World War,* Franklin Watts.

MARSTON, Edward (2009) *Prison,*   Nat. Arch.

WADE, Stephen (2016) *No More Soldiering*, Amberley.

Conscientious Objectors Hansard Nos 12–92

All illustrations are from my own collection of postcards.